The Body Image
Survival Guide
for Parents

What people are saying:

"A must-read for anyone struggling with weight control and body image issues of any kind!! While weight loss centers, extreme diets, TV diet doctors, negative media and the internet may all have caused a great deal of confusion about the way we should look, this book provides realistic and meaningful solutions. I want all my patients to read this before they start any 'diet,' health or wellness program."
Zoltan P. Rona, M.D., M.Sc., author of "Vitamin D, The Sunshine Vitamin"

"This book is fantastic! Seeing a significant increase in eating disorders and body image issues in many girls and boys coming into therapy, I am delighted to see Marci's book. She reveals many real and ongoing struggles that children are experiencing today and provides insight, clarity and techniques to help children begin to identify theses difficulties and overcome them."
Marilyn Strauch, M.A., Psychotherapist specializing in the treatment of eating disorders

"Kids ask tough questions - particularly when it comes to body image, bullying and self-esteem -- and Warhaft-Nadler does not shrink from a single one of them. The scenario-based question-and-answer format makes THE BODY IMAGE SURVIVAL GUIDE a parents' go-to reference at all stages of their children's development."
Sandra E. Martin, Today's Parent magazine, editor

"For anyone and everyone who loves a young person who is struggling with low self-esteem, 'The Body Image Survival Guide' is indispensable. With tremendous compassion and insight, Marci Warhaft-Nadler equips parents to take action and make a tangible, enduring difference in their children's lives. We all want to help our kids feel better about their bodies; this book is the perfect manual to help us do just that."
Hugo Schwyzer, Ph.D., Professor of Gender Studies, Pasadena City College

"Marci Warhaft-Nadler provides parents with specific, practical ways to combat the body pressures that their children face in today's culture. The Body Image Survival Guide for Parents is a must-read for any parent who's been wondering how to help their child build positive body esteem."
Jennifer W. Shewmaker, Ph.D., Associate Professor of Psychology
Abilene Christian University

"This book is a tremendous resource for parents of kids of all ages! Warhaft-Nadler gives parents the script we need to engage our kids in the type of conversations we all should be having. It's an engaging, easy-to-read book that will inspire and encourge healthy self-esteem in everyone who reads it."
Andrea Donsky, Health and Wellness specialist, Founder of
www.NaturallySavvy.com, author of "Unjunk Your Junkfood"

"At the biggest stages of sport as well as martial arts, the greatest strength of an individual lies solely within, and it is precisely due to this reasoning that the boundaries for success are determined or deterred through self-image. I applaud Ms. Warhaft-Nadler for taking on such a task; as a mother, an educator, and victim of diffidence, she brings many important factors for discussion. Ms. Warhaft-Nadler pin-points clearly the determinants of a positive environment, the role each of us play, and the dialogue needed to prevent negative self-image."
Akmal Farah, Canadian National Takewondo team captain

The Body Image
Survival Guide
for Parents

Helping Toddlers, Tweens,
and Teens Thrive

by

Marci Warhaft-Nadler

Eifrig Publishing LLC
Lemont   Berlin

Front cover design and Fit vs. Fiction posters by Ian Darling
Back cover top photo by Sean Gallup, author photo by Stephanie Weiner,
interior illustrations by Rolf Schröter

Printed in the United States of America

Published by Eifrig Publishing, LLC
PO Box 66, 701 Berry Street, Lemont, PA 16851.
Knobelsdorffstr. 44, 14059 Berlin, Germany

For information regarding permission, write to:
Rights and Permissions Department,
Eifrig Publishing, LLC
PO Box 66, 701 Berry Street, Lemont, PA 16851, USA.
permissions@eifrigpublishing.com, 888-340-6543.

Library of Congress Cataloging-in-Publication Data

Warhaft-Nadler, Marci,
The Body Image Survival Guide for Parents: Helping Toddlers, Tweens, and Teens
Thrive
 / written by Marci Warhaft-Nader

    p.   cm.

Includes Quick References and links for downloading materials

Paperback: ISBN 978-1-936172-58-0
Ebook: ISBN 978-1-936172-59-7

1. EDUCATION: Guidance. 2. JUVENILE NON-FICTION: Self-Esteem.
3. Body Image.   4. SELF-HELP: Eating Disorders

I. Warhaft-Nadler, Marci II. Title.

17 16 15 14 2013
5   4   3   2   1

Printed on acid-free paper. ∞

Acknowledgements

I feel incredibly blessed to find myself in the place of recovery, peace, and acceptance that I'm in today. Regaining control over my life and then being able to help others do the same with this book is not something I could have done alone. There are some very important people in my life who deserve a major THANK YOU:

Penny Eifrig (Eifrig Publishing): Thank you for believing in the importance of my message and working as hard as you did to make sure it was heard. Becoming your friend in the process was a bonus!

Melissa Atkins Wardy: You encouraged me to reach a wider audience and inspired me with your own tireless efforts to create a world where kids can be kids whose dreams have no limits.

Hugo Schwyzer, Dr. Jennifer Shewmaker, Dominique Bosshart, Dr. Irwin Cohen, Derek Virgo, Randi Bigman, Rosie Schwartz, Samantha Montpetit-hyunh, and Tracy Moore: I thank you for your insight and expertise.

Ian Darling: I owe you a giant thank you for the time, energy, and talent it took to design my cover photo and Fit vs. Fiction body image awareness posters. I'm truly grateful.

Mickey Held, Lisa Goodman, Laura Landauer, and Reesa Cohen: Thanks for never giving up on our friendships when my struggles made them difficult to maintain. Unconditional love personified.

My Family:

Carol and Leon Aronson: Thank you for loving without judgement and offering support without conditions.

My husband, Rob: I will always be grateful for the way you believed in me when I had stopped believing in myself and for proving that we really can make it through anything.

My kids, Dylan and Logan: Thanks for being a constant reminder of what's truly important in life and for being so darn easy to love!

*This book is dedicated to my mother,
Shirley Mayne, and my brother,
Billy Warhaft, who made sure I felt loved
every minute I had them in my life. I lost you
too soon, but know I was blessed to have you
at all. I hope I've made you proud.*

M. W.-N.

CONTENTS

Forward by Melissa Atkins Wardy

I talk with hundreds of parents every week about issues our children face while trying to grow up in a media-saturated culture that values beauty and style over brains and substance. Time and again, one of the big concerns I hear is the worry parents have about their children and body image. Parents of children ages two to thirty-two have written to me asking for help to restore a positive body image. I have even had people write to me who are not yet parents, but are concerned about the body image of their future children. When we look at the statistics from research showing us just how preoccupied our young kids are with the perceived perfection of their bodies and how young this starts, I think it is safe to say we are at the tipping point on this issue.

Parents are in need of talking points and action items that families can embrace and put to good use. Families need a tool kit to navigate their way through our body-conscious culture in the age of obesity and Photoshop. Poor body image should not be a prescribed conclusion for our daughters, and parents can play a huge role in breaking the cycle of self-loathing. The same can be said for our sons, as we seem to be learning more and more about how the distorted male physique in media is impacting boy's body image. We need to raise a generation of kids who rebuke the messages the media is trying to sell them about their bodies, and instead give our children more meaningful, inclusive, and lasting definitions upon which they measure their worth.

When Marci Warhaft-Nadler and I were first getting to know each other while we were creating a Body Image Workshop for my blog, we had several phone chats scheduled to get a sense of how the other was approaching body image and teaching parents. I think our shortest phone call was just under two and a half hours. It is important to be passionate about your work, and that comes through in the interviews Marci gives and in her writing. I think it is important for your work to resonate with others and to create change, and Marci accomplishes that through her tips and advice.

We are more than the sum of our parts. Parents, families, schools, and communities can start to shift the way we relate to our bodies and how we teach our children to value their bodies. Adults can lead by example and model what positive body image looks and feels like. And that is the key, isn't it? Feeling good in our skin. It really makes life delicious when we can accomplish that!

This book is the tool kit parents have been searching for. In short, it is the conversation we should be having about what we are teaching our kids regarding health, food, and how we relate to our bodies as we travel through life. It has the conversation ideas and projects families can turn into a way of life, just like teaching "please and thank you" and the ABC's. It really can be that simple, but first we have to be willing to get honest with ourselves and how we feel about, treat, and relate to our own bodies. Our children are born full of awesome. Let's make sure they stay that way, and give them the foundation they need to love their body as they grow.

Byline: **Melissa Atkins Wardy** is the owner of *Pigtail Pals & Ballcap Buddies*, a company offering apparel and gifts for children, inspired by the beauty of childhood. She advocates and writes about issues involving gender stereotypes and the sexualization of childhood.

My Journey

Growing up, I was the last kid you'd think would have body image or food issues. I was athletic, confident, outgoing, and generally very happy. I also loved food. I never thought that by the time I was a teenager I would end up using it to hurt myself. I spent years restricting myself from it and then years compulsively overeating it, and I've put my health at risk more times than I can count. The scary thing is that only my family and closest friends knew what I was going through. To outsiders I was in complete control.

My body image issues started with a trauma, as they often do. When I was 17 years old, my older brother passed away from liver disease when he was just 21. When Billy died, a big part of my self-esteem died with him. But I tried to keep that hidden.

I spent 25 years working in the fitness industry as a dance instructor and personal trainer. I spent my days, nights, and weekends telling people how to take care of their bodies, while secretly abusing my own. Telling other people how to eat well and exercise properly was the easy part. Showing myself the same kindness and respect was far more difficult. It took me until my mid-30s to find the courage and strength I needed to recover.

We are living in a society that glamorizes skinny bodies for girls and muscular physiques for boys, and as a result, our kids are more stressed than ever about living up to the images they see around them. After I was lucky enough to find recovery, I created "Fit vs. Fiction," an interactive workshop I bring to schools to tear down the dangerous myths related to fitness and beauty, and empower kids to appreciate themselves for who they are and encourage them to believe in all they can be.

Today, I'm the mother of two amazing boys who have seen me overcome some pretty tough challenges, and I hope they have learned something from the experience. Having been through what I have with my own issues, I am determined to help kids avoid the traps that I couldn't. As a parent, it's easy to feel powerless when our kids are struggling, but the good news is, we are anything but powerless. There are things we can do to help our kids grow up with a healthy self-esteem and positive body image. I want to help other parents not only spot potential problems but also prevent them through open dialogue and activities. The first step is to understand the issues we're facing, and the next step is to start dealing with them. Remembering how hard it was for my mother to watch me mistreat myself the way I did, wishing she had had somewhere to look for answers, I'm hoping to provide parents with the tools they need to help their kids tune out the nonsense and tune in to their own incredible potential.

It took me close to 20 years to figure it out, but one thing I know for sure is that self-worth should not be measured in pounds.

Introduction

Let's face it, becoming a parent can be as scary as it is exciting, and despite our best efforts to be as prepared as humanly possible, there are some situations that you may never see coming.

We expect our kids, regardless of what age they are, to deal with a certain amount of worry now and then, but there are certain concerns that just make more sense than others. Having to reassure your child that you'll be home soon the first time you leave her home at with a babysitter, or spending a few minutes before bedtime clearing his closet of monsters is to be expected, but having to convince your stressed out six-year-old that her nightgown or snowsuit does not, in any way, make her look fat, is not the kind of thing most of us are prepared for.

Gone are the days when it seemed like only teenage girls worried about their weight; now girls and boys as young as five years old are struggling with body image issues. Day after day, kids are bombarded with messages from the media, society, their peers, as well as countless other sources, telling them that they aren't good enough, smart enough, attractive enough, and certainly not THIN enough. As a result, more and more kids are putting their health and lives at risk by engaging in dangerous behaviors to get what they think is the ideal physique.

It's hard to believe, but research confirms that children have adopted society's warped view on body shape and size by the time they are just five years old. One has to wonder how society is finding its way into their young psyches so soon. Are the negative messages of self-judgment sneaking through some window we're inadvertently leaving open, or are they blatantly smashing through the front door? I think it's a combination of both. Some of the messages our kids are getting are loud and clear and therefore easy to spot, but others are much more subtle and even more dangerous because we don't even see them coming.

Kids are struggling. We need to understand the threat that they're dealing with and then face it head on.

As a body image specialist, my goal is to tear down the harmful myths surrounding beauty and fitness and empower kids to love and appreciate themselves for who they are instead of judge themselves for who they think they're not. When I lecture at schools, I hear from kids who are thoroughly confused when it comes to their body image. They're confused about how they're supposed to look, how they're supposed to feel, and who they're supposed to be. It's not easy being a kid in this crazy world we live in and it's even tougher being a parent. I cannot begin to tell you how often I hear questions like:

"What do I tell my daughter when she asks me if she's fat?"
"Why does my nine-year-old son want six-pack abs?"
"How can I tell if my child has an eating disorder?"
"What can I do to make sure my child is getting the healthiest messages at home?"

Like it or not, society is going to be telling our kids a lot of things about themselves that we don't agree with and their messages are going to be loud, so it's our job as parents to make sure our healthy, positive ones are even louder.

Chapter 1

Ages 0-3: Do I look fat in these diapers?

Yes, you read that right. Believe it or not, we need to start building our kids' self-esteem from the very beginning. The facts are beyond disturbing, but unless we understand what we're dealing with, we won't be prepared to deal with the tricky situations that may come up.

Studies show:

81% of 10-year-olds are afraid of getting fat &
51% of 9- and 10-year-old girls feel better about themselves if they are on a diet.[1]
At least 46% of 9-year-olds restrict eating.[2]
Hospitalizations for eating disorders in children under 12 years of age increased by 119% between 1999 and 2000.[3]

As parents, we want to protect our children from the superficial and often judgmental world that awaits them, but it's a task that can feel somewhat overwhelming. The good news is that there is a lot we can do, starting from the minute we bring our babies home, to empower them with a strong, healthy self esteem and to help them grow up with the self-confidence they deserve. While these statistics are scary, they can also be changed. We've finally started challenging society's views on beauty, and I truly believe we're headed in the right direction. Kids need to believe that their self-worth isn't measured in pounds or in someone else's opinion of who they should be because if they can grow up loving and respecting themselves for who they are, there will be no limit as to what they can become.

How do we get started?

When our kids are this young, we are pretty much in control of their environment. We control what they see and hear, and this definitely

---

1 *Mellin, Scully and Irwin, 1991*
2 *Mellin, Scully and Irwin, paper presented at American Dietetic Association Annual Meeting, October 1986. (Berkeley study)*
3 *Agency for Healthcare Research and Quality, April 1, 2009.*

works to our advantage. Here are a few suggestions to help create the kind of environment that will help your kids to grow up loving who they are, instead of judging who they think they're not.

ROLE MODELLING

I cannot say this strongly enough: Little girls learn so much about how to treat themselves by watching their moms (and sisters and grandmas and aunts). It's crucial that daughters see their mothers being kind and accepting of themselves. This can take work, because it's become almost second nature to criticize our jiggly arms or round tummies and we don't realize that these seemingly harmless comments are anything but harmless. As silly as it may feel sometimes, make a point of complimenting yourself, out loud, on a daily basis. Challenge yourself to do so in creative ways. For example: Feel free to look in the mirror and proudly say, *"I LOVE my arms because I use them to lift and hug my baby, to roll out cookie dough and maybe even do a few push ups"* and, *"I LOVE my thighs because I use them to dance with my baby and walk through the park."*

Extend those compliments to your baby by saying things like, *"Oh, look at your strong legs climb the steps!"* or, *"Let's wash those busy arms and feet!"* or, *"Does it feel good to have a tummy full of healthy food?"* or, *"Big Girl! Look how much you've grown since Christmas!"*

Your little ones won't understand the concept of "healthy food" or how much time has passed since Christmas, but they will understand your tone of voice and attitude as you set a framework for how your family will view body image.

By doing this, your child will grow up loving her body for what it can do, not judging it for how it looks. The best part of this exercise is that by committing to just a few seconds of self-appreciation every day, you'll see your own self-esteem increase as well.

Sticky Question: *My three-year-old has a bit of a potbelly and is rubbing it while complaining that she looks fat! What do I say?*
Solid Answer: *Tell her that she's supposed to have a round belly at her age because her body is growing and getting stronger every day. Explain that there are a lot of muscles and organs in her tummy that are*

filling it up and as she gets older, her legs and arms will get longer and she'll get taller and her belly will get flatter. Let her know that you love her belly because it's part of a truly wonderful kid!

IMAGE-PROOF YOUR HOME

We've all heard of baby-proofing our homes: the act of removing any potential dangers our babies may come into contact with. We plug electrical outlets, soften sharp table edges, and lock cupboard doors. Well, now can also IMAGE-PROOF our homes by clearing out the negative messages and replacing them with positive ones. It's a pretty simple exercise actually; just look around your house for magazines, books, posters, or anything that promotes the unrealistic images of beauty that surround us today. Even though kids this young aren't reading yet, they are soaking in everything they see around them, and we need to make sure that what they see is helpful and not harmful.

Believe me, I'm not suggesting that we can put blinders on our kids and keep them from seeing the evils of the beauty-obsessed world we live in, but the fact is if we can show our kids examples of beauty in all shapes, sizes, and forms from the time they are very little, they will be better armed to deal with the superficial and critical messages that start coming their way as they get older. A big part of the body image problem is that kids see impossibly perfect models on TV and in magazines and then compare themselves to these images and walk away feeling inadequate—like they just don't measure up. However, if they have already seen beauty in a variety of forms, it will be easier to understand that the problems aren't with their own bodies, but with the ones they are seeing on TV.

A great thing to do is to use family photos of past and present to decorate your home. Replace the stack of magazines you have with family photo albums. Teach your children that beauty is passed down through families, not by marketers and Photoshop.

MAKE YOUR HOME FAT-TALK FREE

We already know how important it is to avoid criticizing ourselves in front of our kids, but we need to extend that to guests in our homes as well. Kids hear everything. They take it in, process it and then, oftentimes, repeat it. Make sure that people who visit your home understand that any kind of fat or diet talk is not appreciated. It sounds strange, but there are a lot of people, who can't go one full day without mentioning the calorie content of something they've eaten or making reference to their desire to lose weight. As awkward as it may feel at first to tell a friend or family member to quit the diet chatter, they'll probably be happy you did. Most people don't even realize they're rambling on and on and just need someone to point it out. If however, they do feel offended by your request, stand your ground, there are countless other subjects you can be talking about, and anyone who finds it difficult to change gears this way needs to examine his own relationship to food and body image.

TRY THIS!
The "I am...." alphabet game

Repetition is the key at this age. Even if your child doesn't understand your words at first, your positive tone will speak volumes. As they get older, your words will be extremely powerful.

While cuddling with your baby, go through the alphabet and letter by letter, find a positive characteristic to finish the sentence, "I am __."

These characteristics should NOT be about physical traits and should focus ONLY on personality and character instead.

For example:

A: I AM AMAZING

B: I AM BRIGHT

C: I AM CUDDLY or CURIOUS

D: I AM DETERMINED or DARING

E: I AM EXCEPTIONAL

F: I AM FUNNY or FEARLESS or FRIENDLY

Say the words, sing the words, put actions to the words, and just make it fun!

The great thing about your child at this age is that you can never be too silly for them and you still have years before they find you completely embarrassing.

Once your little one is old enough to play along, try taking turns coming up with the positive adjectives.

Chapter 2
Ages 4-8: Do I look chubby in this snowsuit?

In 2009, a study done by the University of Central Florida revealed that nearly half of 3-6 year olds worried about being fat. In 1970, the average age when females started dieting was 14. By 1990, the average age had dropped to 8.

"I don't want to wear my snowsuit because it makes me look fat!" Taylor, 6 years old, told his mom.

For the first few years of our children's lives, we pretty much control their environment by deciding what they eat, watch, and hear. As our kids grow, their toys and media change and carry more mature themes very quickly. (The average age a girl receives her first Barbie? Three years old.) Once our kids start preschool, they become exposed to all kinds of outside influences (classmates, teachers, other parents, or care givers), and it's important that we help them be able to process the examples they're seeing and the lessons they're being taught.

NEW FRIENDS

It can be extremely exciting and even a little scary for our kids to make new friends, and while we wish every new child they came into contact with was a great influence, we know that not all kids can get along or be friends. Sadly, peer pressure starts very young, and it's possible to feel like you just don't fit in, before you even know what you're trying to fit in to!

Preschool and elementary-aged kids may also witness or experience the first time someone is made fun of for how they look. Even at just five or six years old, kids can start comparing themselves to their peers. Recently, the mother of a seven-year-old girl told me that her daughter came home from school saying that she didn't want to be the fattest girl in her class anymore. Another mom told me that her six- year-old son begged her to keep him home from school because he was tired of being the smallest kid on the playground.

It is important to teach our children that it is never appropriate to comment or make fun of another person's body. This is especially true for children, as their bodies are still growing and changing. If your child witnesses teasing taking place, teach them how to be a leader; put their arm around the child being teased, and say simply, *"Ava, I'm really happy to have you as a fun friend."* Let's teach our children how to set the example that everyone has worth, and character is more important than looks.

When it's your child being teased, it can be so hard because our first instinct is to protect our babies. Be careful not to teach them how to play the role of the victim. Validate their feelings, and ask questions about how they think they can make the situation better (maybe with humor or a statement of self-confidence). Review with your child how the teasers are obviously mistaken because your child has a healthy body that looks just the way it should. Go over the fun and incredible things your child can do with her body. Feel free to share an example of a time when you were teased and how you handled it. "When Mommy was your age, a mean girl named Sarah told me my legs were too big and it hurt my feelings. But, I knew that my legs were strong and healthy and thought Sarah probably didn't understand that it's okay for my body to look different than hers. After a little while, we started playing together in the playground and Sarah wasn't so mean anymore."

The hard fact is we have a lot of overweight kids these days. It isn't right for them to be teased for how they look, but we need to be honest about the state of their health. Maybe there are steps your family can take, with the guidance of your pediatrician, to get your child back into a healthier weight range. Focus on how to make healthy choices around food and exercise, so that playtime is more fun and less of a physical strain. When we love ourselves from the inside out and fuel our bodies with healthy food, we look just the way we should.

Sticky Question: *Your son comes from school and tells you that someone at school called him fat. What do you tell him?*

Solid Answer: *There are two ways to handle this. If your child is at a healthy weight say: You're not fat, you're HEALTHY! Sometimes people say mean things, but that doesn't make them true. Bodies come in different sizes. Some are bigger, some are smaller; who cares? If we all looked the same, the world would be very boring. The next time someone calls you fat, just say, "I'm healthy and I'm great just the way I am!"*

If your child is overweight, he needs to understand that he is no less deserving of respect from other kids than anybody else and that nobody has the right to be nasty to him. Explain that he should proud of the amazing kid he is and should let the bully know that making fun of people for how they look just makes himself look bad.

It's also important to put a plan into action as far as getting your child to weight and fitness level that is healthiest for him. Let him know that you love him unconditionally and want him to be as healthy and happy as he can be and will work with him to get him there.

"My 8-year-old daughter often comes home from school and announces which of her friends are on diets. First I ask what the word diet means to her and then try to explain that a healthy diet is full of a variety of foods and isn't about starving ourselves to lose weight." Mitch, 47

How can we explain to kids that healthy bodies can be all types of shapes and sizes? Kids have a very small frame of reference and need to be reminded that they're not supposed to all look the same. Unfortunately, television doesn't help, because most of the kids they see are carbon copies of each other.

An easy thing to do is to take your child on a field trip to your local mall on the weekend when it's pretty busy and just 'people watch' for a while. You're bound to see people of all shapes and sizes with their own unique sense of style. Remember to mention that it's our differences that make us unique and special.

NEW FRIENDS = NEW TOYS

It's easy to decide what we're going to buy for our kids to play with and what we'd rather leave on the shelves at the toy store, but when the play dates start, that control is lost. To some people, toys are just toys, but many of us know how powerful they can actually be.

It's no secret that the Barbie doll has been causing some controversy over the last few years, and with good reason. With all the "evolving" she's supposed to have done, her physical appearance is still unattainable. While the newer Barbie has moved beyond supermodel and beauty queen into careers in business and medicine, they still all have 18 inch waists and live, work, and play in impossibly high heels. Barbie is considered old-school now, as there are many new 12-18 inch dolls on the market perpetuating the "beauty is best" mentality. From tarted-up Bratz dolls to the vixens at Monster High, we can't avoid the fact that our dolls are getting sexier, and our kids are being influenced by them.

Pepperdine University conducted a study involving a group of preschoolers and a choice of two dolls to play with. Both dolls were identical in every way except for their weight, yet nine times out of ten, the girls chose the thinner dolls to play with. An upsetting carryover from this preference is that this behavior tends to continue in the playground when choosing friends.

Another interesting study that was first done in 1961 and then replicated in 2003, involved a group of 5th and 6th graders who were shown six drawings of children and were told to choose the one they would be most likely to play with and the one that they would choose to play with last. The drawings included one child without any disabilities, four children with varying disabilities and disfigurements, and one who was obese. In all cases, the obese child ranked the lowest and the child without challenges was ranked the highest. Interestingly, when the second study was done 42 years later, there was a significant increase between the drawings that ranked the highest and the ones that came in last, proving that kids are becoming increasingly more judgmental when it comes to body shape and size.

Toys should encourage creativity and imagination, not feelings of inferiority and shame.

I am looking forward to the day when dolls really do reflect our real-life population and are as varied and different as we are. Until then, we've got to be creative! Don't let commercials and marketers tell you what your daughter should be playing with. If you do that, all she'll be left with are pink baby carriages and kitchen sets! Kids are full of imagination and curiosity; how we help encourage it is up to us.

Sticky question: *My daughter came home from playing at a friend's house and asked me if she could get some of the cool dolls her friend has. The problem is, these particular dolls make me extremely uncomfortable, because they wear too much makeup and too little clothing. What can I do?*
Solid Answer: *Be straightforward. Say something like, "I'm so glad you had fun at Crystal's house and that you got to play with new toys, but I'm not comfortable with the way they're dressed and think they're too grown up for you, so I'd rather not have them at home."*

Ask her what she likes about them and try to find something similar that you'll both enjoy. You don't want to forbid her from playing with them when she's at her friend's house, but by telling her why you feel they're inappropriate may get her thinking about them in a different way.

"Barbie, I think Ken's on Steroids!"

Girls aren't the only ones who play with dolls—except for boys, they're called ACTION FIGURES.

I can vividly remember being a little girl and watching my big brother play with his G.I. Joe figurine—although his toy was very different than the one for sale today. The original G.I. Joe was created in the 1960s by the Hasbro toy company and was created to look like a regular guy who was believably fit and strong. Today's version looks likes like he should be posing on stage at a bodybuilding competition. Even our beloved Superman has been given a makeover. Apparently, someone decided that he didn't look powerful enough and gave him insanely exaggerated muscles and an impossibly square jaw. For a lot of boys, these dolls, I mean...action figures, represent what a hero is supposed to look like. As a result, I have 9-year-old boys asking me why they don't have rippling muscles as well!

"The worst insult you can tell a guy is that he has no abs and is lanky, bony, or too skinny." Omayd, 17

We need to teach our sons that a truly strong man isn't judged by the strength of his muscles but on the strength of his character.

*How can **we** explain the concept of substance over image?*

TRY THIS!
Everyday Heroes

Start a conversation about the important people in your children's lives; feel free to pull out family photo albums for a visual prompt. Have them talk about the people who make them happy, make them laugh, and help them feel good about themselves. Ask your daughters to name the women whom they look up to and have them explain what is so special about them. Help them understand that these women are special because of WHO they are and not how they look, and they would be just as amazing and inspirational if they were taller, shorter, thinner, or wider.

The same thing goes for the boys: *Who are the men that your son looks up to? Why does he admire them? Do they make him feel safe and protected?* I'm willing to bet that not all, if any, of his male role models possess perfectly chiseled, well-sculpted muscles, and this will help him understand what true heroes look like. Discuss what kinds of people could be considered superheroes in his community; what types of people really do save lives? Why not take a trip to your local fire or police station where he can meet these heroes in person and see how different they look from each other, and as a bonus he'll get to see some heroic women as well!

Now Switch!

Do the same exercises in reverse. Have your son list the important women in his life and discuss how different they may look from each other and then take your daughter to meet her local heroes.

TRY THIS!
Create an "All About ME" Book:
This is a lot of fun and incredibly easy to do. It can be as simple or elaborate as you'd like it to be.

Step 1: Buy a scrapbook (or some interesting paper and bind it together to make a book)

Step 2: Have your children start listing all sorts of facts about themselves. Try to list as many things that you can think of together: favorite song, favorite food, favorite movie, best vacation, funniest memory, etc.

The most important part of this project is that you're doing it together. There's no better way to show your children that they're valued than by sharing your time with them.

The great thing about really drilling home messages about body image for kids at this age is that they still think their parents are brilliant. That's only going to last a few more years, so we need to take advantage while we still can!

TRY THIS!
Make a Sunshine list!
At the end of every day, maybe while enjoying dinner together, ask your children to think of one thing that they feel they did right that day. It can be anything, big or small, like picking a piece of trash off the ground and throwing it in the garbage can, being friendly to a new kid at school or setting the table for dinner. Write these good deeds down on a piece of paper called your "Sunshine List" and hang it up on the refrigerator or wherever it can be best displayed. At the end of the week, take the list down and read it from top to the bottom. When children feel pride in themselves, it encourages them to keep making good choices and by celebrating their positive actions with them, you are reminding them of how beautiful they are on the inside.

Feel free to name the list whatever you think your children will relate to best. Your sunshine list can be called a "Pride list" or a "Feel Good" list or even a "Woo Hoo for ME" List. It's all about having fun!

Chapter 3

Ages 9-12: Do these hormones make me look fat?

"I'm a lot taller than the other girls in my class and even some of the boys, so they call me names like Sasquatch, which hurts my feelings." Jasmine, 11

"A few girls in my class wear bras already, but they have nothing to wear them for. I ask them why they wear it and they say it's because they want to look more attractive for boys. It made me feel like I had to wear one too, but I really didn't want to." Sarah, 10

Last week, a friend of mine told me that her 9-year-old daughter planted her feet in the ground and shouted, "I don't want to grow up!" When her mom asked her why not, she answered, "I don't want to grow up because grownups are FAT and I don't want to be fat!"

Yikes! Where do I begin?

In this case, it was easy to figure out where the fear came from, as she comes from a long line of yo-yo dieters and "fat talk" is commonplace in her household. By seeing the adults in her life focus on body shape and weight, she's started to develop an unhealthy relationship with food and her body. Sadly, this isn't unusual, especially at her age.

The tween years are tough—not just for the kids experiencing them, but also for their parents, who are struggling to find ways to make things a little easier for them. Not only are kids this age still dealing with the same pressures from the media, society, and peers that have surrounded them up to this point, but now they've got the added stress that comes from more homework, possible transition to middle school, exposure to risky behaviors, and, probably the scariest challenge of all, PUBERTY!

"My best friend started to develop way before me. She has a pretty big chest and I'm really small. Sometimes I wish that I looked like her, but then she tells me that I'm so lucky that I'm small and the boys don't pick on me and try to grab me." Riley, 13

Puberty generally occurs between the ages of 8-13, but could start sooner or end later. It's essentially the time when a young girl's body prepares itself for womanhood. While many classrooms discuss most of the changes that kids go through during this time, one area that is definitely not talked about enough is puberty-related weight gain.

Weight gain during this time is not only to be expected, but is also a necessary part of the growth process and the last thing we want to do is impede that process in any way, shape or form. Girls should expect to gain weight, especially around their hips and breasts, and often under their arms, upper back, and waists; but too many of them panic at the first sign of their clothes fitting tighter.

I recently heard from the mother of a 12-year-old girl who was worried that despite the fact that her daughter ate well and was very active, she was noticing some weight gain around her stomach area. I reminded her of what she had just told me about her daughter eating well and being active and assured her that what was happening to her daughter was completely healthy and the worst thing she could do would be to say anything to make her self-conscious about it.

You do not, I repeat, do not want to put your children on any kind of diet while their bodies are doing exactly what they're supposed to be doing, or it could result in a skewed metabolism resulting in a life filled with weight and body image issues. However, it's the perfect time to talk about healthy lifestyle choices.

"How can I explain puberty to my daughter in a way that will make sense to her?" Laura, 42

Kids want the truth, plain and simple, short and sweet.
Puberty actually starts in your brain. The female brain releases a special hormone (GnRH) that travels to the pituitary gland. This gland then releases two more hormones (LH and FSH), and then they all make their way to the ovaries. Once there, the ovaries start producing yet another hormone called estrogen, which is responsible for preparing your body for womanhood and having children. Basically, puberty is part of the transition between being a kid and being an adult.

Make a point of reassuring your daughter that this may be a bit of an awkward time when her body seems to have a mind of its own, and some body parts may be growing faster than others. However, things WILL settle down. The best thing she can do during this phase to help it go smoothly is to live a healthy lifestyle, complete with nutritious food and plenty of physical activity.

Here are some TIPS on how to deal with the tween years, fears and occasional tears:

1. As always, the conversation should never be about weight, but should focus on health. Talk about all the work her body's doing and how important it is to fuel it with a variety of high quality foods that will help it grow in the strongest, healthiest way possible. Explain that her bones and muscles need physical activity to function properly. Puberty is a very emotional time, and we want to avoid making emotional connections with food for as long as we can.

2. Make healthy foods available 24/7. Growing kids are hungry kids, and by making healthier options easily accessible, you can avoid them filling up on empty calories. The easiest thing you can do is keep a bowl of fresh, washed fruit in a bowl on the kitchen table or counter so they can see it when they walk in the room. To be honest, I think sometimes my kids grab the fruit because they can't be bothered to look for anything else, which is just fine with me.

3. During this time, when there can be so much focus put on what their bodies look like, it's super important to make sure you compliment them on their actions instead of their looks. Let them know how proud you are of them and how interesting, funny, intelligent, and fun to be with they are. Make sure they hear you complimenting other people on their actions instead of their looks as well this will remind them that what they do is far more important than how they look.

4. A great idea would be to look through some old photos and find some of yourself during this time so your daughter can see the changes that you went through. Seeing similarities in your experiences might give her some perspective that her body looks exactly the way it's supposed to.

I was definitely a late bloomer. I can vividly remember one day in the sixth grade when a boy named Eric walked over to my desk and in front of everyone, lifted up his shirt and said, "Look Marci, I'm flat too!" I was pretty mortified. I'd be lying if I said I didn't feel a little vindicated when a few months later he asked me to be his girlfriend and I turned him down...flat!

STICKY QUESTION: *Why am I going through puberty before/after my friends are?*

SOLID ANSWER: *Everybody goes through puberty and will experience the same changes, but will do it at their own pace. Some kids may start sooner and may start later, but everyone catches up at the end. There is absolutely no reason to feel embarrassed during this time. It's all a part of growing up strong and healthy. The important message here is that puberty is not something negative to be feared, but something positive to be celebrated.*

Chapter 4

Think body image issues are just for girls? Think again.

The mother of a 13-year-old boy approached me to tell me that her son had nearly gotten suspended from school for calling a girl in his class "fat." The principal explained the rules about bullying and expressed how badly the boy's comment had hurt the girl's feelings. What he neglected to mention was the reason behind why her son had chosen to act out this way and the reason was an important one.

Knowing her son the way she did, she was confused by his comment and asked him to explain. What he told her was that he only called her fat because she and her friends had been teasing him mercilessly about being too SKINNY! They called him names like "wimp" and "skeleton boy." According to their teasing, his arms and legs were too scrawny and weak. He fought back in a way he hoped would get them to stop and maybe even feel as bad as they made him feel. Where was the principal's concern for this little boy's feelings?

It's hard for many people to understand that it's not just girls who feel pressure to look a certain way; these days young boys are dealing with body image to a degree that they never have before. Surprisingly, their pressure is coming from two directions. Some boys are hearing the message that they're too small and not nearly as muscular as they should be, while others are being taunted for being too fat and lazy. It's difficult to feel good about yourself when you're constantly being told that you don't measure up. Teen-based shows and magazines are covered with images of young men with perfectly chiseled six-pack abs and biceps bursting through their sleeves, leaving the average, healthy teen or tween boy feeling inadequate. What they don't realize, of course, is that many of these teen actors aren't actually teens at all, but are in their 20s and even 30s in some cases!

Actor Trevor Donovan played 18-year-old Teddy Montgomery on the series 90210 from 2009-2011. He was 31 years old when he started. Cory Monteith started playing the role of 16-year-old Finn Hudson on the TV show Glee when he was 27-years-old.

Why is this so dangerous?

Think of it this way, if a 16-year-old boy tries to compare his body to the body of a grown man who's just pretending to be 16, he's going to feel inadequate and his self-esteem and self-confidence will drop drastically. What he doesn't realize is that it's a complete waste of time, energy and emotion for him to compare things like his height, weight and muscle mass to that of a full grown adult.

TRY THIS!
Body Swap

A fun way to get this point across would be to flip through magazines and cut out a few pictures of adult males as well as pictures of boys his age. Then cut the heads off of all of them (sounds a little gruesome, but here comes the fun part). Start mixing and matching the boys' faces with the adults' bodies so he can see for himself how bizarre it would look if a real kid had the body of a grown up! Remind him that his body is changing and will continue to change for awhile and the best thing he can do for his body is to take care of it, not waste time wishing it were different.

Interestingly enough, while our boys are hearing the "muscles make the man" message from their televisions, many fashion magazines and runways are saying something completely different. If you look at the average male model of the 1990s, you'll see guys like Tyson Beckford, who were all buff and brawn, and oozing of alpha male testosterone. If you look at what the most successful male models look like today, you'll see a very different physique. Male models these days are under similar scrutiny as their female counterparts to be skinny. In fact, in May 2010, a British mannequin manufacturer was criticized for its latest super skinny male model with a 35-inch chest and 27-inch waist. The manufacturer said they were "simply reflecting the shift to gender blending fashion," but eating disorder specialists feared it would negatively impact the young men they were targeting. It's incredibly frustrating and hard to believe that clothing designers are purposely designing their clothes with unhealthy, undernourished bodies in mind. Speaking of things that are hard to believe, in 2010, popular Belgian model Florian Van Bael was asked to leave the set of a photo shoot for clothing retailer Abercrombie & Fitch when he was caught eating a croissant! Models on this shoot were under strict supervision by agents monitoring what they ate, drank, and how much they worked out. Florian broke the rules and was fired. He may just be the first person ever to lose his job over a delicious pastry! Boys are definitely feeling insecure about the way they look, but we don't hear about it because they don't talk about it.

"I know a lot of guys my age that feel insecure about how they look, but they don't talk about it too much. A kid in my school killed himself last year, and I think it was because of his looks. His arms were smaller than average and the weightlifter kids would make fun of him. It's sad because he was a really nice kid, never got into trouble and his parents loved him a lot. He was 15." Omayd, 17

Women are expected to be emotional and to talk about their feelings, while men are supposed to be strong and silent. Since when did hiding your feelings while giving them time to fester and grow become a sign of virility? Young boys need to be taught that sharing their feelings doesn't make them weak or effeminate.

Hugo Schwyzer, a professor of history and gender studies at Pasadena College explains, *"We expect girls to feel body image issues, but we don't expect it of boys and we don't give them the vocabulary for it. Men can be just as vulnerable as women, but they're not socialized to have the vocabulary to vocalize the pain."*

In most cases, it's so much easier to know what a teenage girl is thinking than it is to try and read the mind of her male counterpart. Usually, if a girl is feeling ugly or unpopular, she'll say straight out, "I'm ugly. I feel like I have no friends." Never something you want to hear from your child, but knowing how she feels will give you the chance to help and offer support. Boys are not as forthcoming. It's not as likely that you'll pass a group of boys and hear them complaining about feeling fat or unpopular.

To illustrate the communication skills of most adolescent boys, I will share the conversation that took place between my 13-year-old son and me the other day. It went just like this:

Dylan: *Mom, do I HAVE to go to school?*
Me: *Of course you do.*
Dylan*: Can I please stay home?*
Me: *No, you can't. It's a school day. Why do you want to stay home?*
Dylan: *I don't know.*
Me: *There must be a reason.*
Dylan: *I just don't like it.*
Me: *Is there something going on at school that's bothering you?*
Dylan: *No.*
Me: *Would you tell me if there was?*
Dylan: *No.*
Me: *Really? You wouldn't tell me if something was wrong??*
Dylan: *Nope. But there isn't anything wrong.*
Me: *But you just told me that you wouldn't tell me if there was!*
Dylan*: Yup.*
UGH!

For parents, it can be tough to know the difference between regular teen angst and something more serious, which is why we need to provide our boys with the tools they need to express what they're feeling and to ask for help when they need it.

Professor Schwyzer explains, *"We don't fix young women's problems by pretending that boys have none. We won't minimize girls' issues by addressing boys' issues."*

When boys grow up hearing that they need to "man up!" or "suck it up!" They get the message that men need to be tough, and if they don't feel tough, they'd better fake it. As a result, they tie their self-esteem into how strong they look. Aging can be challenging for men because strength and virility often come with youth. So, as a man ages, he may feel tremendous pressure to stay as youthful looking as possible.

In 2011, a new ASPS (American Society of Plastic Surgeons) statistic showed a "sizeable increase in facelifts and other surgical procedures in men." Their 2010 statistics showed that more than 1.1 million men underwent cosmetic surgery with the top 5 surgical procedures being:

1. Nose reshaping
2. Eyelid surgery
3. Liposuction
4. Breast reduction in men
5. Hair transplantation

You'd expect to see this type of thing in the entertainment industry where no one is left unscathed when it comes to criticism over appearance, but surgeons are reporting that they're getting more and more office visits from "regular Joes" who just want to look younger. With men and women becoming more equal in the workplace, one theory is that the last area where men feel superior to women is in physical strength, so if they start to feel that they're losing their youthful machismo, some men will go to great lengths to get it back, even if they have to pay for it.

It's time to teach our boys that self-worth isn't measured by the amount of weight they can bench press at the gym!

Here's a tip: If you really want to make your son uncomfortable, sit him down, look him in the eye and say, "We need to talk." Then continue by asking, "How are you feeling? " I can almost guarantee you'll get nothing more than a simple, "I'm fine," as a response. For some reason, face-to-face chats usually do not work for boys, and you have a much better chance of getting him to open up if you're doing an activity together. I find that my boys are the chattiest when we're playing basketball together or even driving somewhere. So feel free to start a conversation when you're folding laundry, driving to soccer, or making dinner and then let the conversation flow.

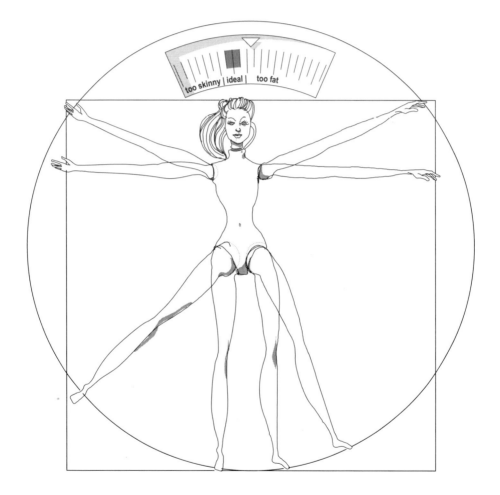

Chapter 5
Ages 13 and up: Teen years = increased body fears

53% of 13-year-old girls are unhappy with their bodies.
78% of 18-year-old girls are unhappy with their bodies.
The number one wish of girls 11-17 years old is to lose weight.

"There are statistically significant relationships between low self-esteem and a number of anti-social or negative behaviors such as drinking, drugs, eating disorders, sexual promiscuity and poor academic performance." Dr. Irwin Cohen, Criminologist at the University of Fraser Valley.

When I first started bringing my "Fit vs. Fiction" workshops to schools, many people advised me to stick to elementary schools because it would be a waste of time to talk to high school kids about body image and eating disorders. The general opinion was that by the time children reached high school, they were already too set in their ways to be helped. Plus, by that time they usually believe they know pretty much everything there is to know and we, as their parents, know absolutely nothing. However, this is the time when they need our help the most; they just don't realize it. Having developed my own eating disorder when I was 17 years old, I can say from experience that it is never too late to intervene. How much could I have benefitted from self-esteem based programs at that age? Hard to say, but I wish I had gotten a chance to find out. It's important to reach out to kids of all ages, to never stop reaching out. Because how they feel about themselves, and how much they believe in themselves, will greatly influence the goals they set and how likely they are to achieve them.

It's ALL about their friends
This is the time when our kids' friends really take over as primary influencers in their lives. Most teenage girls and boys are desperate to fit in with their peers, and if they don't, it can seem like the end of the

world. Four years can feel like a lifetime if you're spending it struggling to be who you think people want or expect you to be.

Allison, the mother of a 15-year-old girl, says that her daughter stopped eating breakfast when she entered high school. None of her friends ate breakfast and she felt like a "pig" when she was around them. In high school, kids think it's cool to be just like everyone else, and it's not until they're a bit older that they realize that it's even cooler to be different and unique.

17-year-old Sharayah admits that high school has been very difficult for her: *"I used to be fine about the way I looked until I got to high school. In grade 9, I was on the chubbier side and started starving myself to fit in. There were about six girls in my group of friends and four of us were restricting our food and constantly on diets. Being a teenager and being in high school has been the toughest four years of my life. I won't even walk around my house in a pair of shorts and a bra, because if I see myself in the mirror, that will be the end of my day. It doesn't matter how many pounds I lose or how many people tell me I look good, I still feel the need to be perfect."*

Joanna, 16: *"A friend of mine used to drink nothing but tea all day and then at night, when her family was asleep, would sneak into the kitchen and binge on pizza and whatever leftovers she could find. She never ate proper meals and was constantly trying to lose weight. I couldn't understand her obsession with her weight. I mean we were only 13."*

Something that often gets overlooked when it comes to body image is the fact that skinny girls can get teased too. While we live in a world where many people believe that there's no such thing as TOO thin, a lot of girls are picked on for being just that.

Lori shares her experience: *"My childhood was miserable. I was a walking skeleton who ate like a pig and could not gain weight for anything. I was teased for years. I had a teacher who confronted me at school about being anorexic when I wasn't. I still feel a deep wound from that all these years later. I sought help from my mom and she didn't know what to do. Skinny kids have body image issues too sometimes."*

Sadly, we have become somewhat brainwashed by the digitally enhanced images we see in the media that we have almost forgotten what real girls look like. I find it completely ridiculous when I pass by a billboard with the picture of a model who looks completely emaciated yet still manages to have large, heaving breasts. I'm not saying that it never happens, but full, voluptuous breasts on a painfully thin frame is certainly not common. Sadly, naturally skinny girls with proportionate measurements can become victims of teasing because they aren't seen as curvy enough! Apparently, it's not enough to be thin anymore, now women need to be thin while also having an ample bosom and perfectly round butt.

It's easy to assume that thinner kids don't struggle with body image issues and that assumption can be dangerous.Some kids feel the need to start overeating or consuming artificial weight gaining drinks in order to put on extra pounds and that needs to be discouraged. The best advice you can give your child in this case is to keep eating in a normal, balanced way and let her body take care of itself. If your child tells you that she's being harrassed by her friends or kids at school, explain that it's not her body but the attitudes of the critics around her that needs to change. Make sure she understands that bullying is never acceptable and often comes from a place of insecurity.

Go ahead and speak to the school as well and let them know what's going on so they can offer her support when she's there. If the hurtful comments are coming from an authority figure, you absoluetly need to intervene since it can be difficult for kids to understand that sometimes even adults speak out of ignorance and that just because the harmful words are coming from someone they are supposed to respect, it doesn't make them true.

Another thing we need to be conscious of is that while it's fantastic that we're starting to see an increase in television and print ads supporting more realistic body shapes for women, as with the Dove Campaign for Real Beauty which celebrates women with softer, curvier bodies, we can't inadvertently snub women who aren't as curvaceous. In 2002, the movie "Real Women Have Curves" was released starring actress America Ferrera about coming to terms with her body image issues. Since then, I've heard that sentiment a lot, and while it sounds empowering at first, it can actually be somewhat exclusive. Some women are thinner while some are more voluptuous, but we are all "REAL" and need to grow up appreciating and respecting each other for our similarities as well as our differences.

Communication is Crucial

Kids need to feel accepted, even if it means doing or saying things that make them feel uncomfortable just to feel like part of their peer group. Anytime there's a sudden change in behavior around food or their bodies, it's immensely important that parents know where or whom the sudden changes are coming from. While we can't change other people's kids, and believe me, sometimes I wish we could, we have to make sure that our kids are constantly being reminded that they matter, that their opinions and their feelings are valid and respected, and that doing the right thing may not be the same as doing the popular thing. But it's always the best choice in the end.

Many teenagers find the idea of opening up to their parents less than appealing, but don't let that stop you from trying. Just keep it simple. Ask about their friends and their friends' hobbies; find out what they're interested in. While the idea of a house full of teenagers can be a scary one, making your house a comfortable place for your children and their pals to hang out is a great way to meet the kids who are probably having the greatest influence on yours.

Even though your kids may not be ready to talk, make sure they know that you are always ready to listen. Just knowing you're there for them will give them a great sense of security.

Stick to your word. As soon as your child comes to you for help, make her the absolute focus of your attention. Television's turned off, book's closed, work's put aside. It's not just about hearing their words, but also listening to their feelings. Resist trying to tell her what to do, and instead work together to come up with short and long term solutions that will help her feel supported by you but also give her a sense of responsibility for herself.

Joanna, 16, shares: "*I used to have an eating disorder due to excessive bullying from a guy at school. I was bulimic. It went on for years. I complained to my teachers and the school principal but nothing happened because the kid was a school favorite. One teacher even told me to grow a thicker skin because I was too sensitive. I still resent her for that.*"

Parents: If the teachers won't listen and the principal looks the other way, go to the school board. And if they won't help, keep looking until you find someone who will. Our kids need to see us fight for them; it lets them know that they are worth fighting for!

Joanna continued: "*I think that being in a small school and having a different body type than other kids around me, I was just asking for it. I mean, being different in a school with a small population puts a huge target on your back. I'm much better now though. I eat well and exercise three times a week. Plus, I have good friends and a great boyfriend who love and support me.*"

Contrary to what they'd like us to believe, kids need one-on-one time with their parents. It doesn't have to be a lot of time; in fact, even taking just a few minutes every day to connect will send them a message that you're always going to be there for them and that they're a priority in your life.

TRY THIS!
Lunch date
If your child eats lunch at school, choose a day to pick her up and take her out for a change. A little unexpected attention goes a long way.

THERE'S A **0.002%** CHANCE HE'LL BE A **DOCTOR.** THERE'S MORE THAN A **50%** CHANCE HE'LL THINK HE **NEEDS** STEROIDS TO ATTAIN HIS IDEAL BODY AS A TEEN.

Forget the false bravado: kids are losing the self-confidence and self-esteem they need to tune out the negative messages all around them. The good news is that we can still inspire our kids to be who they want to be, and not who they think they're supposed to be.

Fit ·vs· Fiction

Self-worth should not be measured in pounds

FITVSFICTION.COM • TWITTER.COM/FIT__VS__FICTION • FACEBOOK.COM/VISITFITVSFICTION

Chapter 6
Life outside of school

School can pretty much be the center of the universe for most kids, since it is where they spend most of their time and find most of their friends. But what happens when their friends aren't being as friendly as they should be, or school just seems tougher than they'd like it to be? That's when after school activities can be invaluable.

The list of benefits related to children engaging in extracurricular activities is an important one:

Self-confidence
Support
Responsibility
Contribution

There is something incredibly empowering about finding something that you love to do and discovering that you're good at it.

Self-confidence

Encourage your kids to try out all kinds of activities until they find something that they truly enjoy doing. There are endless activities for kids to get involved in and part of the fun is finding out which ones they're best suited for. It's important that you don't choose the activity for them, but help them choose the one(s) that gives them the most joy. Do your kids like playing sports? Maybe they're interested in art or music. How about a drama class or nature club? The possibilities are endless! The feeling of pride that comes from excelling at something you enjoy is hugely fulfilling and necessary when building positive self-esteem. Believe it or not, we don't even have to be good at something to gain self-esteem from it, since sometimes the pride simply comes from being able to try something new and unfamiliar.

Support

When all of our children's friends come from the same place, then all of their influences do as well, and that's not always a positive thing. Our kids need to learn how to value and appreciate themselves without looking for constant validation from their peers, and being involved in out of school activities can be a great way to do that. Having friends outside of school gives them an extra source of support when they need it.

"When my son would come from school feeling horribly depressed after being bullied all day, having soccer and Martial Arts to go to several days a week gave him a new group of kids and teachers to connect with. Being part of a team and hearing positive reinforcement from his teammates and coaches gave him the confidence he needed to believe in himself and stand up to his bullies." Kim, on her 11-year-old son

Studies show that kids who participate in sports find it easier to resist peer pressure when it comes to engaging in dangerous behaviors involving things like drugs and alcohol.[1]

Boredom can be risky. For some kids, having too much time on their hands with nothing to do can send them looking for excitement where they have no business looking. Giving your children somewhere safe to be, with people who have similar interests and goals can help guide them and keep them moving in a positive direction.

Matthew, 40: *"When I was in high school, I loved playing baseball and being on the school's baseball team. I truly believe that it was being on the team that helped me stay away from the trouble some of my other friends got into. There were times when I'd be at a party where there was alcohol and I KNEW that if I were to drink and get caught, I'd be kicked off the team and that was enough to keep me away from it. It's funny, but in my high school a lot of kids just didn't understand someone not wanting to get drunk, so by saying that my coach would kill me if I did, gave me an easy out and kept me from having to defend my choice to stay sober. Also helpful, was the fact that my teammates weren't drinking either, so I didn't feel so alone."*

1 Arch Pediatr Adolesc Med. 2003;157(8), 733-738.

Responsibility and Contribution

When you're part of a team, you learn very quickly that you're not only responsible for yourself but also for the other players, which is a great way to teach the concept of being just one part of a bigger picture. It's important to be on time for practices and to be supportive of your teammates. Learning responsibility at a young age can help your child be better prepared for school and even her career as she gets older.

Some kids excel at team sports, others prefer individual activities; the key to building confidence through activity is to help your child find whatever it is that he likes to do and then support him in continuing to do it. Be prepared, because that support may involve cheering for your daughter while sitting on a cold bench, freezing your buns off in a hockey arena for what feels like hours on end, or maybe covering every last wall of your house with your son's artwork; but trust me, they'll love you for it, and, most importantly, they'll love themselves.

Olympic Bronze medalist, Dominique Bosshart, was the first Canadian athlete to win a medal in her sport of Taekwondo, at the 2000 Olympic Games in Sydney, Australia. She spoke to me about how being involved in sports helped take her from troubled kid, to world-class athlete: *"When I was little, the kids at my school were incredibly cruel to me. I was taller and bigger than a lot of the other kids in my class and they called me all kinds of names and made fun of my size. I hated going to school and started getting into a lot of trouble. I was growing into a somewhat angry teenager, who saw things as unfair and hypocritical. One day, my brother joined a Taekwondo school and made me go with him. My coach said, "If you train hard then maybe one day you can go to the Nationals." I was like, "Sign me up!" I needed that encouragement because I didn't get it at school academically or in any other sports. Starting taekwondo and getting positive feedback was instrumental. It was as though I just needed someone to take notice, to inspire an idea, for someone to make me feel like I could do something special."*

There are so many different ways to get your kids involved in activities outside of school and trying different things is all part of the experience. Sometimes we think we know which activities our kids will be drawn to and then are surprised when something completely different gets them excited. Open them up to all the options that are available and then stand back and let them lead the way. The fun part is in watching them discover new skills and interests that neither of you were aware of before!

Extracurricular activities can motivate, inspire and strengthen the self-esteem of any child, from artist to athlete and everything in between:

ART

Whether it's drawing, painting or sculpting, art classes cultivate curiosity while improving concentration and coordination. By giving kids a great place to express themselves, they learn how to be creative without worrying about the end result. Besides, art is messy and who doesn't love getting messy?

MUSIC

Music classes can help kids have an easier time with schoolwork as it teaches them how to absorb and remember information. Learning how to play an instrument can be challenging; facing and overcoming the challenge will spark a huge boost in self-esteem.

DRAMA

Being able to perform in front of an audience enhances the type of confidence that can help any child as he or she gets older. Being encouraged to use imagination and collaborate with others can help with problem solving and social skills. Drama classes also give the opportunity to work through emotions in a positive, creative, and safe environment.

DANCE

Taking dance classes can improve overall health, flexibility, balance, strength, coordination, and stamina. The educational benefits include discipline, creativity, and focus and are another great way to learn how to express feelings and emotions.

SPORTS

Team sports give kids a chance to meet friends who have similar interests and can help teach things like teamwork and leadership skills. Individual sports help create a deep sense of self-reliance and confidence. Being active reduces stress and depression and improves motor skills and strategic thinking. The great long term pay off is that regular exercise at a young age increases the chances of continuing an active lifestyle as an adult.

MARTIAL ARTS

Girls and boys can learn a lot from the training they get through whichever form of martial arts they decide to try. Some popular choices are: Karate, Judo, Jujitsu, and my personal favorite, Taekwondo. Both of my sons have been training and competing in Taekwondo since they were barely five years old, so I've been able to see for myself the benefits that this type of activity can offer.

Most martial arts are very physical and will improve overall fitness levels, while also teaching important skills like self-defense and self-discipline. There is a high degree of respect that is taught during training, for oneself and for fellow students, teachers, and parents. A strong sense of pride and confidence comes from the perseverance it takes to master new techniques and earn each new belt in their color belt ranking system. This is a great way to learn how to respect your body for what it can do, rather than what it looks like.

GIRL SCOUTS / BOY SCOUTS

Any activity where kids get to be with other kids and experience new things while learning how to give back to their communities is always a great one. With groups like the Girl Scouts / Boy Scouts or the Boys and Girls Club of America, kids learn skills like leadership, teamwork, and commitment. A healthy sense of self-esteem comes from the feelings of competence and belonging that these groups instill. When you believe that you're an important part of a community, you want to do your part to improve it, and this type of program gives kids the tools and confidence they need to succeed.

The goal here is to encourage our kids to try new things and discover unknown talents, while making new friends and learning a few things here and there. One thing that can't be overlooked, however, is that with all the benefits that come with taking part in group, team or individual activities, there can also be some risks.

With so many programs to choose from, there are a few that require parents to be a little more vigilant than others when it comes to making sure that their kids are getting positive, healthy messages from their environment, coaches, and teammates.

"When the pressures of sport competition are added to cultural ideals that emphasize thinness, or a certain body type, the risks increase for athletes to develop disordered eating." National Eating Disorder Association

Certain sports, for example, are connected with higher risks of body image and eating disorder issues because they focus on appearance and on the individual instead of the entire team. Sports like dance, gymnastics, and figure skating place a significant level of importance on how their athletes look, and glorify thin, muscular physiques. Since we're talking about kids, you'd think this wouldn't be an issue since no child should be judged on how her body looks in a leotard. They shouldn't be, but they are. Even young kids can find themselves being compared to others and as a result, may start feeling insecure and uncomfortable with themselves.

"I really believe that my body image problems started when I became a dancer at 4 years old. Dancers and gymnasts are expected to be skinny, have muscles and literally look perfect. I was chasing perfection every single day, in the studio and in the gym, not only in my ability but also with my body. Many girls I know, including a good friend of mine, used to self-harm because of negative comments they would hear about their bodies. Even today, my coaches refer to me as the fat girl because my ribcage doesn't stick out, my legs aren't stick-thin, and I even eat more than 200 calories at dinner. Sexualization is also a big thing in competitive dance and many times I find myself questioning

the moves I'm doing or the costumes I'm wearing and wonder why the people who do the most inappropriate moves get the highest scores. The very first time I performed a male/female duet with inappropriate movements and clothing I was eight years old." Sharayah, 17

Claudia shares a different perspective: *"My daughter Amy is 12 years old and has been dancing for nine years. Dance has given her lots of confidence and poise. She can also handle school presentations because she's used to being on stage and enjoys it. Her level of fitness, athleticism and flexibility has improved as well as an appreciation for her body and how it works. There are a couple of girls who are more developed and who I catch looking at themselves in the mirror in a judgmental and obsessive way, who usually don't wear the bootie shorts that most of the other girls wear and choose sweat pants instead. In ballet, all the girls wear tights and bodysuits and I can tell it makes some of the girls uncomfortable when it's viewing week and the parents are allowed to watch. I see how issues of weight and size are an issue for some kids, but certainly not all of them."*

We trust our kids' coaches and instructors to be positive influences, we expect them to protect our kids and guide them towards their goals, and I believe that for the most part they share the same goals as our children. However, intention and result can be two different things. The biggest trophies and shiniest medals mean nothing if they come at the expense of our children's self-worth. It is crucial that there is open communication between parents and coaches and that as a parent, you feel 100% comfortable approaching them with any concerns you may have. Children also need to understand that if at any time, they feel the least bit uncomfortable with their instructors or how they're being instructed, the right thing to do is to bring these feelings to their mom or dad.

Coaches, instructors, and group leaders may be experts in their fields, but you know your child best and if at any time you disagree with how your child's being taught or coached, you need to speak up immediately. Every teacher has her own personality and style of teaching, and while we can't expect to love all of the teachers who work with our kids throughout their lives, there are times when our gut instincts tell us that we need to intervene, and that's a feeling that shouldn't be ignored. I definitely suggest trying out an activity a few times before signing up long term, and there's nothing wrong with trying out several places until you find the right match for you and your child.

It's ridiculous that today's athletes not only have to be highly skilled at what they do, but they also have the added pressure of needing to LOOK good while doing it! Sports Illustrated did a great job of reducing successful female athletes to mere sex objects when they featured three of them in their 2012 Swimsuit issue wearing nothing but PAINTED ON SWIMSUITS. Alex Morgan (U.S. women's soccer), Natalie Coughlin (U.S. Olympic swim team), and Natalie Gulbis (LPGA) all stripped down to their birthday suits in order to have bathing suits literally painted onto their bodies. Let me get this straight, Sports Illustrated, first you feature models wearing swimsuits and now you feature athletes NOT wearing them? Here's a crazy idea: Why not show female athletes playing sports?!

Female athletes aren't the only ones trying to balance image and performance; too many young boys are also getting the message that talent and skill will only get you so far, if you don't have the good looks to match.

Take a look at some of today's most popular athletes: soccer's David Beckham, baseball's Derek Jeter, and football's Tom Brady. Are they talented? Sure they are, but I can pretty much guarantee that it wasn't Beckham's skill on the soccer field that landed him his own underwear line with retail clothing company H&M.

This pressure to look "like an athlete" has some young boys hitting the gym and the heavy weights before their bodies are ready for it.

Derek Virgo, strength and conditioning coach at Bill Crothers Secondary School for Active Living and Sport in Ontario, Canada explains: *"While it's perfectly fine to start weight training by age 12, the goal should not be muscular size but muscular strength and endurance. Too many young kids are focused on the muscles they see, which I refer to as, "Mirror Muscles," than the muscles they use. These kids are setting themselves up for disappointment and are actually impeding their success by expecting physical results their bodies aren't capable of achieving. A young kid who trains 4-6 weeks, for example, will not see a change in his muscle mass, but will see a change in muscle strength, and this is the concept that most boys struggle with."*

This is another example of how important it is to get to know the people who are coaching your kids. While Derek's approach is focused on long term athlete development and encourages building well rounded athletes that aren't just stronger but are smarter as well, there are some coaches who tend to see past what's best for the individual athlete in order to get the best results for the team. The prize becomes more important than the person.

Talk to the coaches. Do not be intimidated and be direct.

They need to understand that under no circumstance should your child be put on any kind of extreme workout or diet regime without your consent. The important message here is that getting your kids involved in activities outside of the school environment is incredibly beneficial on their physical and emotional health. Children who are given ample opportunity to play, learn, and create in a nurturing environment alongside their peers will grow up understanding confidence, courage, and determination and will be able to use these character traits for the rest of their lives.

Top 5 things to ask your child's coach/instructor, group leader
1) How important is winning to you?
2) What will my child learn from this experience?
3) If I have any questions or concerns, what is the best way for me to reach you?
4) What type of supervision is provided?
5) How can I help?

Once we are satisfied with the answers we get, we need to stand back and give the coaches space to coach. A truly successful kid is one who has all of the people around him working TOGETHER to be supportive and encouraging.

THERE'S A **0.003%** CHANCE SHE'LL BE A **LAWYER.** THERE'S A **42%** **CHANCE** SHE'LL WISH SHE WAS THINNER BY THE TIME SHE GETS TO THE 3ᴿᴰ GRADE.

It's sometimes hard for us to see, but kids are losing the self-confidence and self-esteem they need to tune out the negative messages all around them. The good news is that we can still inspire our kids to be who they want to be, and not who they think they're supposed to be.

Fit ·vs· Fiction

Self worth should not be measured in pounds

Chapter 7

How to help your overweight child

"My daughter is bigger than a lot of her friends, and I worry that she's going to be teased because of it. I would like her lose weight and be healthy but don't want to make her feel any worse about herself than she already does. What do I do?" Karen, mother of an 11-year-old daughter

The very first thing parents need to do if they feel that their child is overweight is to find out for sure. Sadly, our society tends to underestimate the sizes that healthy bodies can come in, and all too often, children will seem overweight just because they're bigger than some of their peers, when in reality, they're within a perfectly healthy weight range. Make an appointment with your family doctor or pediatrician, without your child being present, and find out if there really is any reason to be concerned. If your doctor confirms that losing weight would, in fact, be a healthy option, then find out what a healthy range would be. Be careful not to get too hung up on numbers though; a scale can't tell you how fit, energetic, and happy your child is. You can see that in how she talks about and carries herself on a regular basis. Remember, our goal is to focus on raising healthy kids, not necessarily skinny ones.

Consulting dietician and writer Rosie Schwartz shares: *"When parents call me to make an appointment for their child, I explain that while I am more than happy to meet with the parents, I will not discuss weight or diets with their kids. The parents are in charge of what the child eats, and it's not something that the child should be focusing or worrying about."*

Whenever parents ask me for advice on what to say to their overweight children to help them lose weight, my answer is simple:

Nothing. Say nothing. Research tells us that talking about and focusing on weight with our kids will not end in the desired effect that we're hoping for and can actually make the situation worse.[2]

While there is nothing we should be *saying* to help our kids improve their health, there is a lot that we could be *doing*. First and foremost, keep things POSITIVE. It is important that your children understand that healthy bodies come in many different shapes and sizes and that you are proud of who they are and that they should be proud of themselves as well.

There is a lot of stigma that comes with being overweight in our society, and often, even if a child loses the extra weight, he still might feel shame and embarrassment because being overweight had become a part of who he is. It's as if he can't see himself any other way. It's our job as parents to help them strengthen his self-esteem along with his body. We all want healthy children, but by micromanaging their digestive systems and telling them how to eat all the time, we aren't letting them understand the messages their own bodies are sending. Our bodies are amazing machines that work really well if we let them. But if we try to manipulate them through unhealthy dieting, we're setting ourselves up for trouble long term. Let your kids learn how to listen to the cues their bodies are sending them. They need to be able to tell when they're hungry and when they're full. If we keep telling them how, what, and when to eat, they'll never learn how to listen to their natural instincts around food and will grow up eating for reasons that have nothing to do with hunger, which is why so many of us turn to food to deal with emotional issues.

STICKY QUESTION: *Mom, do I need to go on a diet?*
SOLID ANSWER: *Nope. Diets aren't healthy. But we can all start making healthier food choices so we can fill our bodies with ingredients that will make us feel a whole lot better.*

The very last thing you want to do is put your child on any kind of restrictive diet.

---

2 2007 Wellness Councils of America

"Adolescent girls who diet are at 324% higher risk for becoming obese than those who do not diet." (National Eating Disorder Information Center)

Food should not be thought of as "good" or "bad." Food is just food. The problem with demonizing certain foods is that we tie too much emotion around them. We don't want our children to judge themselves on the foods that they eat. If we teach our kids that cookies are bad and then they eat a cookie, they'll start thinking that they're bad because of it—and that is exactly what we're trying to avoid. We spend so much time worrying about the calories our kids are taking in, and not enough time working on how many calories they're putting out.

The key ingredients in helping an overweight child become a healthy one are encouraging a healthy attitude around food, promoting positive feelings about them and their bodies, engaging them in an active lifestyle, and providing family support. Remember, kids learn more from what we do than what we say, so try these tips for raising a healthy child:

Make it a family affair

The last thing you want to do is single out one kid with special food or portion sizes at meals. Instead why not change the way the entire family eats? The goal is to be serving healthier meals in healthier portions and everyone can benefit from that. Remember, you're not putting your child on a diet, just making some changes to how and what you all eat.

Keep food talk positive

It's not about the foods you take out and all about the foods you bring in. We all get in to a sort of comfort zone where we seem to pick up the same type of foods week after week, so try something different. Go ahead and try out some exotic looking fruit you've seen at the market hundreds of times but never considered actually bringing home, or try a recipe swap with a friend as a way of adding to your weekly menu repertoire, keeping in mind that you're looking for healthy options.

Menu plan and shop with your kids

Allowing kids to get involved in choosing menus and then taking them along to shop for the ingredients will give you a great opportunity to teach them how to read labels without being fooled by clever marketing. Don't stop there; let them help you cook the meal as well! Creating a meal from scratch can give your children a new kind of respect for and pride around food. We spend too much time being afraid of what we eat and not enough time enjoying it.

Get creative with Theme Nights!

How about "Japanese food night" or "Breakfast for dinner"? Only your comfiest pajamas are allowed at the dinner table on those nights. Eating healthy shouldn't be seen as a punishment, or a chore, but as a fun and delicious way for us to honor and nurture our bodies.

Get active TOGETHER

Exercise has an incredible number of benefits and will help us keep our weight down and our energy up! If group activities are where your child feels the most comfortable, SIGN HER UP! Regular physical activity with a group of friends will help keep her motivated and interested.

If team sports or sports in general are not your child's thing, there are tons of other ways to stay active, but it may take a little creativity on your part. When my boys were a little younger, we would walk over to the park in my neighborhood, and I would come up with obstacle courses for them to run by using whatever equipment I could find. I'd say things like, "Run up the yellow slide, do five jumping jacks, slide down the red slide, skip over to the bench, step on and off the bench five times, do a crazy dance and then run to the basketball nets and back!"

An added bonus is that by demonstrating the courses, you'll be getting your workout in too! Make it even more interesting by letting your kids come up with an obstacle course for you!

Throw a dance party in your living room! Let your kids play DJ by putting on their favorite tunes while you all dance around until you're completely boogied out! The moves don't matter ... just get moving.

The object is to make exercise so much fun, they'll never even know they're getting fit!

Keep things going after dinner. Instead of settling in on the couch for the night, go for a walk. The television will be there when you get back. Take a stroll through your own neighborhood, or explore somewhere you've never been!

If bad weather is keeping you inside, you can always sneak some physical activity into your TV time. Challenge your kids with a fun dare like, "I dare you to do a silly dance whenever a commercial comes on!" Very few kids can refuse a good dare.

Don't be afraid to slip on a pair of hiking boots, strap on a bike helmet, or make up your own wacky sport, just get moving as a family and you'll all be better for it.

Support their hobbies

Are you raising aspiring artists or musicians? Take an interest in whatever interests your children and be supportive. They may be feeling a lot of pressure about how they look right now, and it's a great idea to involve them in something that is skill-based and not image-based.

Don't let them see you worry!

If you make their weight a big deal, then they'll make their weight a big deal, and all that worry won't help anyone.

STICKY QUESTION: *"Mom, am I fat?"*

SOLID ANSWER: *The first thing you need to do is find out where the question is coming from and how it's making her feel. You also need to be honest. If your child is overweight, then she may be looking for help and not a simple answer like, "No, you're perfect just the way you are."*

Ask her WHY she's asking that and what that word means to her. If she is being teased at school it's important to deal with that quickly and directly. Go ahead and speak to her teachers and make sure they know that any kind of bullying won't be tolerated. It's also a great idea to ask the teachers what kind of education the kids get about bullying and about accepting people who may look different from them. Next, make sure your child knows that nobody has the right to make her feel bad about herself and explain that the problem is with the bullies and not with her. Let her know that the kids who are usually the meanest are usually the ones who are also the saddest and since deep down, they don't feel very good about themselves, the only way they can try and make themselves feel better is by hurting somebody else.

Eleanor Roosevelt said it best when she said, "No one can make you feel inferior without your consent."

You can reply: "Why do you ask? How do you feel? You're not fat, but you are bigger than some of your friends, and that's okay and nothing to be embarrassed about. But why don't we start getting even healthier together? It'll be fun having more energy, and it'll feel great to see ourselves get stronger!"

Do what you do best: Love your child.

Feeling loved, respected, and appreciated by you will teach her how to love, respect, and appreciate herself. It's when we like ourselves and know that we deserve to be happy that we make healthy choices in all aspects of our lives.

Chapter 8
When mom or dad needs to lose weight

Karen, (mother of 15-, 13-, and 8-year-old daughters) asks: *"I've decided to lose weight and get into better shape. How can I make changes to my lifestyle and my body without making my kids feel self-conscious about their own?"*

Deciding to make healthy lifestyle changes is a positive thing and the perfect opportunity to explain to your children how important it is to treat our bodies with the kindness and respect they deserve. Be clear that you are not changing your diet or physical activity in order to fit into a pair of jeans or look better in a swimsuit, but to enhance your quality of life.

As always, keep things positive. Instead of criticizing your body for the flaws you may see, focus on all the things that a healthier body will be able to DO. Try approaching the subject by saying, "I'm not feeling as strong or energetic as I'd like to feel, so I'm going to start feeding my body with the foods that will give my body all the good stuff that it needs and I'm going to start being more active." Be excited about it! Also, you want to avoid talking about how you're eating LESS. If they notice that you're eating smaller portions or avoiding going back for seconds or thirds, simply explain that you're just listening to your body and you feel that you've had enough.

Keep in mind, that it's all about progress, not perfection. If you miss a workout or eat a little more than you had planned, DON'T make a big deal about it. Our kids need to see that perfection is unrealistic and that the goal is not to be perfect - just perfectly happy with whom we are.

STICKY QUESTION: *"A little boy in my daughter's class walked up to her while I was standing there, looked at me, then back at her and said, "My mom is skinny!" I had no idea what to say.*

SOLID ANSWER: *Simple is best. Just say, "Some moms have blonde hair, some have brown hair, some moms are smaller and some are bigger, but we're all moms and we all love our kids to the moon and back!" It's not your responsibility to educate him on the subject of diversity and how people come in various forms; you can leave that to his parents, along with manners and respect. Your job is to make the situation comfortable for your own child and by turning an awkward situation into a positive one that will show her a self-confidence she can learn from.*

I talk a lot about the importance of liking yourself. In general, we tend to be kind and patient to the people we love around us, yet judge ourselves harshly for every perceived flaw we have or mistake we make. As someone who spent way too many years hating how I looked, how I felt and who I was, I can tell you that this type of self-judgment is pointless. It's amazing how much more we can accomplish if we just give ourselves the chance to be a little human.

This whole, "Love yourself, no matter what" concept has some people confused. I have had a lot of people challenge me, by asking, "So, you think people should like themselves no matter how much they weigh?"

I answer, "YES."

They continue, "Even if they are overweight?!"

I answer, "YES."

They continue disapprovingly, "It's OKAY to like yourself if you're OVERWEIGHT?? But that's not healthy!"

At last, my chance to explain: *"Liking YOURSELF is not the same as liking or accepting WHERE YOU ARE."*

I truly believe that a person's value as a human being does not change regardless of what the scale says. We're no less deserving of love and respect from ourselves or others if we're underweight, overweight, or at our goal weight. But that doesn't mean that we need to stay at that weight.

The truth is, we tend to be kinder to and more patient with those we love. So if we love ourselves, we will WANT to be as healthy and happy as possible and will then make better lifestyle choices.

Chapter 8: When mom or dad needs to lose weight

Hating ourselves for who we're not will get us nowhere, but respecting ourselves for we are, will remove any self-imposed boundaries on who we may become.

If we really want to help our kids grow up believing that they can be anything and anybody that they choose to be and that the best body they can have is a healthy body, we need to believe it for ourselves as well.

Chapter 9

Womb for rent

"I just had my second baby and am working on losing the extra weight I gained during pregnancy. How can I explain my weight loss to my daughter in a positive way?" Laura, 42

This is another great opportunity to talk about how amazing and miraculous our bodies are! Explain to your daughter that while you were pregnant, your body had a big job to do as it was creating her little brother or sister. While the baby was growing, your body also needed to grow to make room for him/her and you needed to eat more to make sure that you had enough energy to take care of yourself, the baby and the rest of the family.

Go on to explain that now that the baby's here, your body still needs lots of energy, but will get it in a different way. Avoid saying things like, "I need to get back into shape," or, "I need to lose my belly." You want her think of pregnancy as the wonderful experience that it is and not connect it to feeling lousy about yourself. Talk about the fact that when you were pregnant, your body was taking care of the baby from the inside and now that the baby's here, your body will start taking care of the baby from the outside.

Gina, 31, shares: *For me, the changes to my body were very welcomed. My husband and I both really loved watching my belly get bigger, and I even felt more beautiful when I was pregnant. I have always felt that pregnancy was a beautiful thing, the bigger the better! But I do remember being taken aback by how many people at my work would only comment on how well I was "carrying the weight" and how I was "All baby," and stuff like that. I knew it was meant to be a compliment, but I found it strange that it's the first thing people think to say because they assume that all women want to hear how thin they look. One woman at work even said, "You're so lucky, some women just let themselves go when they're pregnant and then it's hard to get their bodies back later." Personally, I never struggled with my pregnancy weight gain or felt self-conscious about the changes my body was going through, but I definitely noticed that there were people around me who perceived pregnancy as less than beautiful.*

Keep in mind: There is no rush. Only TV moms give birth one week and are itsy-bitsy-bikini-ready the very next.

This brings me to the topic of celebrity pregnancy weight loss.

Dealing with the changes that go on in our bodies when we're pregnant can be challenging at times, but we need to reassure ourselves that our bodies are doing exactly what they're supposed to be doing in order to give our babies everything that they need. Once these little people arrive and our bellies are no longer renting out their space, accepting our super soft tummies isn't always easy. What can make this transition even more challenging is when we see female celebrities giving birth and then walking along the red carpet just a few weeks later, wearing barely-there outfits, looking as svelte as ever! We can't help but wonder, "If they did it, why can't we?"

Victoria Beckham did it, so did Miranda Kerr and Jamie Pressley. In fact, it's what all the hot celebrity moms are doing. They're all delivering their babies and jumping into their string bikinis just a few weeks later. What is it about being famous that makes it possible for these women to shed their pregnancy pounds so quickly and seemingly easily, while the rest of us "regular moms" usually spend those first few weeks in our most forgiving lounge pants and oversized shirts? What is it about fame that enables these women to join the mommy club while simultaneously holding on to their "Hot Chick" status without skipping a beat? Do they know something we don't? Are they privy to some well-guarded secret that allows their bodies to remain virtually unchanged through one of life's biggest transitions? Perhaps they are just more strong-willed than we are, with superior willpower and dedication?

Maybe, but I don't think so.

In fact, I think we've got it all backwards. Maybe the key to real beauty after childbirth resides with us "regular" moms. In our society, we have a seriously superficial view of beauty. We're constantly shown images perpetuating the idea that the longer the hair, the tinier the waist, the more perfectly applied the makeup, the better. But as any woman who has raised children will tell you, there may be several times in her life when she sought perfection in her looks, but those first few weeks postpartum were not some of them. Motherhood is messy—a fact that most new moms are willing to accept, along with very little sleep, no time to shower, and spit-up stained clothing. But it's that acceptance and willingness to forgo their basic grooming rituals that makes motherhood so magical and so truly beautiful. Those famous moms who grace the covers of magazines and who discuss at length, the exact diet and workout plan they followed to return to their pre-baby bodies are missing out on what's really important. Is it arrogance or ignorance that has them believing that other women even WANT to be like them? In my opinion, these women are seriously misguided.

Several celebrities are all too proud to share their post-baby diet tips. No sooner do they pop their babies out are they on the cover of magazines explaining in detail, how their personal trainers had them enduring grueling four-hour daily workouts, while following some insane cabbage soup diet or master cleanse, in an effort to repair their bodies from the "damage" they'd done during pregnancy. Not to mention what they won't tell us, like how many of them are requesting tummy tucks during their C-Sections. Are we really supposed to think of them as role models? I remember those first few weeks after childbirth, when I was incredibly tired and just remembering my own name was a huge accomplishment. When combing a brush through my hair and managing a little lip-gloss was a triumph worth celebrating. The sheer thought of adding lengthy workout sessions and starvation into the mix didn't seem like a sensible thing to do. Choosing to focus what little energy I had on my weight would have seemed misplaced.

I honestly believe that we have forgotten the miracle that childbirth is. Show me a woman who has tried unsuccessfully to conceive, and I'll show you a woman who would joyfully trade her flat stomach and narrow hips for the stretch marks and expanded rear end that can accompany a post-pregnant body. Pregnancy is an experience that affects a woman's body, mind, and soul from the minute she decides to conceive. Once pregnant, she then spends nine months growing a HUMAN BEING in her body. Once that baby is born, it's time to enjoy this new journey that we're on, to take care of our babies and ourselves. I resent being made to feel like as soon as the baby has left my womb, my priority should be getting my body back to its pre-baby state.

What exactly am I supposed to be hiding? If pregnancy isn't a crime, then why do I have to hide all the evidence? Since when did looking like a mom become a bad thing? Mothers are amazing people. We work 24 hours a day, 7 days a week, and will accept hugs and kisses as payment. We run households with the type of organizational skills that would put most high-powered CEOs to shame, and instinctively know how to fix a broken toy, soothe a scraped knee, or mend a broken heart. And many of us work other jobs as well. I assume we're supposed to envy those famously fabulous moms for looking the way they do, but instead I think it's kind of sad. It can't be easy. Being a public figure means leaving yourself open to constant criticism from complete strangers. Try to imagine what life would be like if every time you left your house there were millions of people just waiting to tell you how terrible you looked. Celebrities are certainly under A LOT of pressure to be picture perfect all the time, but while I understand why they may feel the need to go to extremes to lose their extra weight in a hurry, I would love for them to at least be honest with how difficult a process it is. There's nothing I find less inspirational or motivating than seeing an interview with a ridiculously thin, brand new mommy and hearing her credit her super lean physique to simple long walks and drinking a lot of water. I would be thrilled to read an interview where the celebrity mom says, "I'm starving and I'm tired. This is what I feel the need to do because of the career I'm in, but it is not something I would recommend for other women." Being perfect isn't inspiring, being human is.

The truth is, the little person we've been waiting nine months to meet couldn't care less about killer biceps or washboard abdominal muscles, but instead are comforted by the softness and warmth of their mommies who are choosing to spend time with them instead of their treadmills.

There is absolutely nothing wrong with a woman wanting to feel good about her body after childbirth. After all, she'd been renting it out for close to a year and deserves to feel great about herself again. My only point is if a woman is taking care of herself, listening to what her body needs, and allowing herself time to enjoy this new and exciting phase of her life, she will be in a much better place to make healthy diet and exercise choices when the time is right.

Celebrate every curve, you've earned them!

Tracy Moore, a Canadian television journalist and host of lifestyle magazine CityLine on CityTV, experienced two pregnancies in the public eye and understands the challenges that can come from being a pregnant celebrity. Tracy shares: *"I grew up in a home where education and athletics were much more important than appearance and as a result, grew up feeling quite comfortable with myself and my body. It wasn't until I got into journalism that I realized how much of an emphasis was put on physical appearance. The pressure to fit into the image that was expected of female journalists in front of the camera did bring out some body image issues, and I found myself restricting what I ate and watching the scale more often than I would have liked. Luckily, I figured out that while appearance played a big role in success on television, it didn't have to come at the expense of my health or self-esteem, and I found a weight that was right for me.*

Being pregnant while hosting a TV show was an interesting experience. I quickly realized how unrealistically pregnant women were being portrayed on television. At times, I felt like an alien while my body went through the natural changes that pregnancy brings, because it just wasn't as glamorous as our televisions will have us think. It was tough because people expected me to look a certain way, and I didn't want to disappoint them by not living up to their expectations. I wouldn't think twice about getting pregnant in front of the camera again. Society's obsession with beauty and thinness wouldn't affect the important choices in my life, but I do know that there are people who would be ready to judge or criticize. To this day, the number one question I get from viewers of my show is, 'How did you lose the baby weight?' I think it's important for people to see what pregnancy can look like for real women with real babies growing in their bodies, so that we can be more kind and understanding to ourselves and other women."

I think part of the problem that new moms have when it comes to feeling good about their bodies is the lack of time they have to spend on themselves. Weight-loss programs and TV commercials tell us that in order to feel confident again, we have to make big dietary and exercise commitments that new moms just don't have. But sometimes, all it takes is just a few small changes at a time to get us where we want to be. I've asked two highly skilled personal trainers to share some tips to regaining the strength and confidence we may be lacking soon after delivering our babies.

Samantha Montpetit-Huynh, owner and founder of Core Expectations, Toronto, Canada's only full-service wellness team providing in-home personal training to pregnant women, offers this advice: *"It's important to start slowly. As much as you may be dying to get the extra weight off, it took 9 months to put it on, so be patient. Eat well and often.*

Make sure you have healthy snacks on hand, like pre-cut veggies, whole grain crackers and nuts, for when you've let too much time go between meals and need to grab something quickly. Try to eat a protein, carbohydrate, and fat, plus a snack at each meal, to keep your blood sugar levels steady and avoid crashes.

For exercise, start with 15-20 minutes of walking each day (if a vaginal birth) and increase a few minutes every week. Strength training can be done 2-3 times a week for 10-20 minutes at a time. Listen to your body! If you've had a C-section delivery, it's best to wait until your 6-week checkup before starting any formal exercise routine. You're not just recovering from your workout, but also from pregnancy and delivery. It's important that you don't forget your core muscles. Even while you are lying in the hospital bed, you can start working those pelvic floor muscles and connecting again. Your transverse abdominals also need to be engaged especially in the early weeks while the uterus is contracting and trying to get back to its original size. Doing gentle isometric exercises that help to get the transverse and pelvic floor working together is your best bet for combating any pelvic floor dysfunction (i.e. incontinence) and treating abdominal separation.

Randi Bigman-Mori, Certified personal trainer, Nutrition and Holistic Wellness coach adds: *"If you're nursing, be aware that cutting back on calories might hurt your milk supply so make sure you're eating enough of high quality foods. If you're like many new moms, you'll be spending a lot of your time at home, so turning your living room into a fitness center is a great option! Your baby can make a great piece of equipment. Just lifting him/her up is strengthening your muscles. Or hold them on your belly while you do crunches. Go for long walks with the stroller, or just dance around your kitchen to your favorite music while holding your baby close.*

If you need more of a challenge, a small investment can get you a stability ball, a couple of light weights, and a mat. There are also some great workout DVDs you could use while your baby is napping. Check out parenting magazines for suggestions or even your local library.

Exercises like leg lifts and knee bends are a good place to start. Also, remember that when you work your abdominal muscles, you need to strengthen your back as well. A few simple back exercises with some light weights will do the trick.

Be social! Once you and your baby are ready to get into a routine, look for community centers that offer mother and baby fitness classes. The supportive environment will provide a fun place for you to get fit with your baby while socializing with other moms. When you take care of your insides, your outsides take care of themselves!

A FUN ACTIVITY FOR PREGNANT MOMS AND KIDS:
Beautify your Belly Bump!

More and more pregnant woman have started painting their tummies as a fun way of honoring their expanding bodies instead of hiding them. Some say that belly painting started from an old world tradition of having body art applied to signify a life-altering experience. While you can have the artwork professionally done, an even better idea would be to make it a do-it-yourself activity with your kids. Grab your little ones, some pregnancy-safe finger-paint, and have your kids decorate your belly with whatever designs their creative minds can come up with. Once your belly art is complete, it's their turn! If you've got one child, you can do the decorating, if you've got more than one, they can take turns being the artist and the canvas.

We often spend too much time trying to avoid looking at our stomachs, or looking at them with disdain, so it's great to be able to engage them in an activity that helps them feel connected to their bodies in such a positive way. Use this time to comment on how special our bodies are and how they perform miracles every single day. Try to point out that while your tummy is busy growing them a little brother or sister, their bellies are equally as amazing because they are unique and special packages that hold all their bones and muscles and all the things they need to do anything and be everything they could ever imagine.

Don't forget to take a lot of pictures to turn into a collage to later share the experience with the eagerly anticipated new sibling!

Chapter 10
Does mom/grandma always know best?

It's estimated that by the time a girl is 17 years old, she's seen approximately 250,000 messages from the media telling her what she's supposed to look like. Now think about how many messages her mother's heard, and how many her mother's mother has heard! That's a lot of messages from people who don't know us, telling us who we need to be.

Being a role model can be tough, especially when it comes to food and body image, but it's a role we automatically take on when we become parents.

How many times have you lectured your kids on the importance of inner beauty, between sips of a diet cola or bites of fat-free cookies? How many times have you assured them of the importance of not following the crowd, while you yourself were following a diet program on the advice of a girlfriend or some celebrity you saw raving about it on TV? Let me give it to you straight: *Your kids are less interested in what you're saying and are more interested in what you're doing. And believe me, they are watching.* Long gone are the days of, "Do as I say, not as I do." Most kids are in a hurry to grow up. When they're eight they want to be 10, when they're 10 they want to be 16, and when they're 16 they want to be 21. Lucky for us, there's nothing they can do to speed up the aging process, but they will however do their best to act as if they can. On their quest for maturity, they will try to emulate the adult with the most influence in their life, and that, my friends, is you. It's been proven that young women are more influenced by their mothers than the media. What this tells us is that we have the opportunity to reach our kids in ways we may not even realize. When your kids see you making healthy lifestyle choices, like taking part in a physical activity on a regular basis or eating a full, balanced diet, they are more likely to do the same. Likewise, if you let things like fatigue, a busy schedule or the fear of trying new things keep you on the couch, and the ease of convenience has you reaching for foods high in fat, calories, additives, and preservatives that temporarily comfort rather than nourish, your kids might follow suit. However, as dangerous as inactivity and unhealthy food habits may be, it is just as dangerous to go to the other extreme and let a diet mentality motivate every choice you make. If every bite and every step you take are based solely on how it will affect your waistline, you are desperately in need of balance. You cannot expect your kids to grow up enjoying a healthy relationship with food if they've seen their mom live off diet products and food scales. You can't teach anyone how to live a healthy lifestyle if you aren't living one yourself.

As parents and grandparents, we have to make sure that our own fears and insecurities around food and body image don't get passed on to our kids. The last thing we want is for our kids to grow up hating their bodies and fearing food. Make sure that you understand what it truly means to have a healthy body and that you aren't letting society's skewed perception of beauty influence the way you speak to or even in front of your child.

We all want to do and say the right things.

No one wants to purposely mess up their kid, and yet, even the best of intentions can lead to dangerous situations if we're not careful. A parent's love should be unconditional. Home should be the one place where we know that we will always feel safe and supported, yet, for some people, it's anything but. Often, in an effort to protect our kids from harmful situations, we unintentionally end up hurting them ourselves.

Obesity is a hot topic these days. Everywhere we turn, we hear messages telling us that our kids are too fat and too lazy and that it's ALL OUR FAULT. We feed them too much and let them play too little. As a result, we've become fat-phobic. Instead of learning what constitutes a healthy diet and ample exercise, we are going to great lengths to make sure our kids don't get fat! The problem is that our fear is being filtered down to our kids and instead of teaching them how to eat food properly, we are making them feel the need to restrict it, and they are growing up feeling that being thin is the key to happiness and success.

I will never forget, a few years ago, when I was speaking at an elementary school and a little girl came up to me and said, "My mom told me that if I don't lose weight, I'll be bullied in high school."

My heart sank. She was in the fourth grade.

This mother was obviously concerned about her daughter's well-being, but in an effort to protect her from a potentially humiliating situation, she was actually creating one herself. Seeing your child in pain, whether it's emotional or physical is the toughest thing for any parent. But, we have to be careful not to let our own fears affect their self-esteem.

First of all, this little girl's body is expected to go through a lot of changes during the four years leading up to high school, and doing anything to alter those changes wouldn't make sense. If the mom really believed that her daughter needed to lose some weight, then it's a belief she needed to keep to herself. It would be up to mom to make HEALTHY, positive lifestyle changes concerning diet and exercise, without bringing attention to it.

What really bothered me about the comment was that it gave the potential bullies too much power. Instead of letting her child know that bullying was wrong, she was telling her to change herself in order to please them. Teaching kids to change who they are in order to be accepted and liked is never a good idea. If our self-esteem was supposed to come from other people, it would be called "Others-esteem" instead!

When we become parents, we have to expect that how we raise our kids will be heavily influenced by how we, ourselves, were raised. Our childhood experiences have a definite impact on the types of parents we become. For some of us, our parents are role models for the type of parents we hope to be, but for others, they represent a dysfunction they'd like to avoid. What's really important is that we learn from all of our experiences and let them help us make the best decisions we can for our kids. The truth is we all seek approval from our parents. Regardless of whether we're 5 years old or 35 years old, we all yearn for our parents' respect and approval and it can be extremely damaging when we can't seem to get it.

In my own life, I was blessed with a mother who constantly made me feel loved and protected. She was warm, loving, and encouraging, and it's hard to imagine that the home she came from was everything but.

Sadly, my grandparents were emotionally abusive, and as a result, my mother didn't grow up with a strong, confident sense of who she was. Fortunately, she did grow up knowing that she wanted to be the type of mother she didn't have, but always wanted.

Interestingly, her parents had a hold on her until the day she passed away from cancer at 56-years-old. She still sought their unconditional love, but never got it. While she wasn't always strong enough to stand up to them for her own sake, she never hesitated to let them know that their judgment and negativity would not be tolerated around her children. It was difficult watching my grandparents be less-than-kind to my mother, but it was reassuring for me to see her stand up for her kids. By defending me, she let me know that I deserved to be treated with respect.

I'm actually amazed by how many women have approached me for advice on how to deal with the way their own mothers and fathers are affecting their children's self-esteem. It's a cycle that needs to be broken, and it's a tough one to break.

Michelle, mother of 2: *"I've never told anyone this, but when I was six or seven I was staying with my grandparents for the weekend and I accidently overheard my grandparents talking about my weight. My grandpa was saying to my Grandmother about how I needed to start watching what I ate more because I was starting to get fat and my grandmother agreed with him. Pathetic as it sounds, it was a defining moment in my life. Here were two people that I loved, who were supposed to love me unconditionally, talking about me like I wasn't good enough because of how I looked. I still tear up when I think about it. The crazy thing is that looking back on my pictures I wasn't fat in the least; I just didn't walk around sucking my stomach in like adults do."*

Jean, 35: *"I can vividly remember being at a family gathering when I was about 8 eight years old. The table was filled with delicious food, and I went to take something to eat. My aunt pointed at me and said to my mom, "Look at her, she's eating AGAIN!" My aunt was so cruel and my mom felt the need to react, so she walked over to me, slapped my face, and told me to stop eating. The sad part is, I don't even remember eating very much that day."*

Karen, 34: "I grew up the 'chubby' one. At mealtimes, in front of the whole family, my mother would say, 'That's enough, don't take anymore! Do you realize how many cookies you ate?!' My house was always stocked with cookies, so I felt like I was constantly being set up for failure. It makes me sad when I hear my mother refer to herself as a 'fat slob' and I try hard not to do the same thing in front of my own kids."

Mara, 45: "My mother made a big deal about it, always criticizing me, and she never reinforced any kind of healthy eating. She just told me that I was big or that I looked fat, or that she looked fat."

Michelle continued: *"I started dieting in middle school, oftentimes with my mother who has been long obsessed with being a size 8 again. We did every diet there was: Atkins, South Beach, raw foods, low carb, low fat, low cal, etc. My mother also did lots of "cleanses" and juice fasts, which held me in the belief that I wasn't clean enough on the inside. By the time I was 13, I was starving myself/bingeing and purging. At one point while out with friends I passed out twice from low blood sugar and smashed my face into a door while falling over. Things got drastically better for me once I moved out after high school and wasn't under her pressure or listening to her negative self-talk all the time."*

Criticism is never a good motivator; neither are shame or guilt. We need to be teaching our kids that it's not our bodies that need to change, but our negative feelings around our bodies that do.

Susan, 43, shares what it was like growing up with an overly critical mother: *"I grew up with a mother that was overly concerned with weight; her own and everyone else's. I feel that it was her constant negative comments that encouraged my issues. When I was a kid, I was always active, always playing outside, always playing some kind of sport, nevertheless, my parents nicknamed me, "Pillsbury Doughgirl." When I gained weight in freshman year at university, my mother bought me a stuffed bear and told me it reminded her of me, because I waddled when I walked because I was fat. She thought it was very funny."*

The comments didn't stop as Susan got older: *"When I was pregnant with my first baby, my mother told me that maybe I'd get lucky and the baby would suck all of the fat out of my body and I wouldn't gain any weight."*

Interestingly, studies have shown that when parents focus their attention on their children's weight and put too many restrictions on what they eat, the risks of these children becoming overweight actually increases. Oftentimes, the restricted foods become MORE appealing and instead of avoiding them, kids end up hiding them and eating them in private, later on. Putting the focus on weight loss, can also result in a child feeling like their parents just don't feel like they'll ever be good enough unless they lose weight, which leaves them with damaged self-esteem and at risk for lifelong struggles with eating disorders. Diets don't work, they just create unhealthy relationships with food and these relationships are incredibly difficult to break away from.

"My family religiously watches shows where there are doctors talking about how to lose weight. Then they constantly repeat what they heard to me and try to copy everything that they were told to do. I understand that they want to be healthy, but hearing them talk about the TV doctors all the time gets annoying!" Hayley, 15

STICKY QUESTION: *My mother was tough on me about my weight growing up and now she's starting the same thing with my daughter/ son. How can I get her to stop making negative comments without hurting her feelings?*
SOLID ANSWER: *Be honest and be firm. There is absolutely nothing wrong with saying, "You know mom, Jessica is a healthy, happy little girl and we want her growing up to love herself and her body so we don't allow any kind of negative food or body talk around us. I know how much you love her, so I'm sure you understand."*
While it would fantastic to be able to solve the problem without anyone's feelings getting hurt that just might be unavoidable. The fact is your mom may feel a little insulted at first and that's okay. Protecting your child is your first priority, and if you show your

mother that this is something you're very serious about, chances are she will at least try to be more sensitive with her comments. If, however, you find that her unsolicited "advice" is still free flowing, tell her that she needs to keep the comments to herself or wait until she can speak with you in private. But criticizing your child and undermining your way of parenting is just not going to be accepted.

If a comment has been made in front of your child, make sure you clearly contradict what's been said and calmly express your own positive feelings on the subject to your child. The point of this isn't to start an argument and it shouldn't turn into a long debate. But, since you can't take back the negative words that have been said, you need to replace them with words of encouragement and acceptance. Any time your child sees you stand up for an issue you feel is important it empowers him with the courage to do the same thing.

The more unconditional support our kids can have around them, the stronger their foundation will be. If our goal is to raise happy, well-adjusted children, we have to work together to make it happen.

TRY THIS!
GENERATION CELEBRATION

Moms, the first thing you need to do is invite your mom and daughter(s) to play along. Next, have everyone collect images and/or a list of names of influential women from their generation. These women can be famous or people they know from their own lives. The emphasis should be on finding women who have had a positive impact on the people around them because of what they do or what they stand for, not because of how they look. Give yourselves some time to do some research. Set a day and time to get together and share what you've found.

One by one, describe whom you've chosen and why. Describe what it is that make these particular women stand out. Use this time to discuss the ways in which society's view of women has changed over the years and also the ways in which it hasn't. This would be an excellent time to talk about the fact that while it's important to have positive role models in our lives, it's equally as important to grow up and become them ourselves.

DON'T FORGET YOUR SONS!

Of course, your son can also play this game with the men in his life. It's just as necessary for our boys to understand that the men who made the most meaningful contributions to this world weren't worrying about the size of their biceps or broadness of their shoulders, but were standing up and fighting for causes they believed in, and he can too!

Since every family is different, the players can change depending on what works in each scenario. Moms can share this activity with their sons, and dads can play along with their daughters. The encouraging messages are the same, regardless of whom they come from.

Chapter 11
The dangers of negative body image

We've talked a lot about all the things that can affect our self-esteem and body image, but what exactly are we dealing with?

The Merriam-Webster dictionary defines body image as: "A subjective picture of one's own physical appearance both by self-observation and by noting the reactions of others."[3]

Basically, our body image is how we think we look and how we let other people make us feel about the way we look. How we actually look can have very little to do with it. Sadly, how we feel about our outward appearance can have a significant impact on all aspects of our lives. The better we look, the better we feel. And the more confident we are to try new things and accept new challenges. When our looks don't seem to measure up, our confidence suffers and we're less likely to accomplish whatever goals we may have set for ourselves.

For kids, we know that society, the media, their teachers, their friends and even their families, have the power to influence how they see themselves. But what happens when the negative feelings become overwhelming and the way they feel about themselves starts controlling how they treat themselves?

"Over one-half of teenage girls and nearly one-third of teenage boys use unhealthy weight control behaviors such as skipping meals, fasting, smoking, vomiting and taking laxatives." (NEDA: National Eating Disorders Association, 2008)

Not everyone who struggles with negative body image will end up with an eating disorder, but it definitely increases the risks. Eating disorders are incredibly complex and difficult to understand for the people dealing with them as well as the people around them. For

---

3 Source: www.merriam-webster.com/medical/body%20image

parents, hearing their kids constantly putting themselves down can be frustrating, especially when it seems like there's nothing they can say or do to change the way they feel. If a child starts developing an eating disorder, parents can feel even more powerless and it's important to understand that while it's not up to a parent to "cure" the disorder, it is necessary to educate themselves about them so they can have a clearer idea of what their child is going through.

There are three very common misconceptions about eating disorders:

1. Eating disorders are about food: Believe it or not, eating disorders are not about food. Food is the weapon that we use to hurt ourselves, either through extreme restriction or overeating. But it's not the cause.

For many people, it starts with a need for CONTROL. Oftentimes, something is going on in their lives that makes them feel like things are completely out of their control and in an effort to feel safe, they try to control the one thing they can; which is their bodies. These feelings can stem from any kind of stress they may be dealing with. Some could be related to a personal trauma they've experienced, relationship issues, stress at school or family issues.

Sadly, it doesn't take long for that sense of control to disappear and the eating disorder to take over completely.

"Growing up, my mother drank too much. And there was a lot of fighting and screaming. She left a few times to stay at a hotel. She scrawled a suicide note on the counter once. My sister moved out. My parents sat me down to say they might divorce. There was this feeling of instability, of uncertainty, and probably most of all as a teenager a feeling that my family was different than everyone else's families. More than anything, I wanted to be like everyone else. So that's the image I tried VERY hard to portray. I was extremely successful at school. Top of my class. I was involved, a leader, outgoing, athletic. Prom queen. Years later, even my closest friends told me they never had any inkling of what was going on at home. I am no longer in school, so I can't be "perfect" through my performance at school. However, I can be "perfect" in my appearance, my body, my strict

diet and exercise regimens. A counselor helped me understand that this is my adult way of doing just what I did as a teen. It's as though everyone will think my LIFE is perfect if I LOOK perfect. It's a shield to keep people from knowing that I struggle with the demands of being a wife and mother. I feel overwhelmed and unfulfilled at times. Things aren't always how I pictured them to be. But as long as I strive toward that image of perfection and in my case through my BODY then I can fool everyone into believing that everything is FABULOUS." Hope, 37

2. You can tell who has an eating disorder by just looking at them:
If only it were that easy. Not everyone who's overweight or underweight has an eating disorder and not everyone who has an eating disorder is overweight or underweight. There are so many factors that make up an eating disorder aside from a person's weight, it's important not to dismiss suspicions you may have strictly because someone may not look ill.

3. Eating disorders are just a way of seeking attention
Nope. When children are hurting themselves through their behavior with food, they aren't just looking for attention, they NEED it. This is not the type of thing that will go away if it's ignored; it will just get louder and more damaging. Act now!
Eating Disorders are defined as: Any of several psychological disorders characterized by serious disturbances of eating behaviors.

The most commonly known eating disorders are:
Anorexia Nervosa, Bulimia and Binge Eating.

Anorexia nervosa: Anorexia nervosa is characterized by emaciation, a relentless pursuit of thinness and unwillingness to maintain a normal or healthy weight, a distortion of body image and intense fear of gaining weight, a lack of menstruation among girls and women, and extremely disturbed eating behavior. Some people with anorexia lose weight by dieting and exercising excessively; others lose weight by self-induced vomiting, or misusing laxatives, diuretics or enemas.[4]

4 National Association of Anorexia Nervosa and Associated Disorders (ANAD): www. anad.org; from the Latin for "Nervous loss of appetite" Encyclopaedia Britannica kids.

Bulimia: Bulimia nervosa is characterized by recurrent and frequent episodes of eating unusually large amounts of food (e.g., binge-eating), and feeling a lack of control over the eating. This binge eating is followed by a type of behavior that compensates for the binge, such as purging (e.g., vomiting, excessive use of laxatives or diuretics), fasting and/or excessive exercise.[5]

Binge Eating Disorder: Binge Eating Disorder (BED) will soon join the ranks with Anorexia Nervosa (AN) and Bulimia Nervosa (BN) as an "official" eating disorder. Binge Eating Disorder is in fact a distinct entity—not just the extreme overeating that plagues many Americans. Binge Eating is characterized by insatiable cravings that can occur any time of the day or night, usually secretive, and filled with shame. Bingeing is often rooted in poor body image, use of food to deal with stress, low self-esteem and tied to dysfunctional thoughts.[6]

These are just three examples of how issues with food can have a serious effect on our lives, and even though there are differences between them, many of the signs and symptoms are the same.

How can I tell if my child could be developing an eating disorder?

These are just a few examples of some of the signs your child could be displaying if they're struggling with an eating disorder:

PHYSICAL:
Weight gain or loss
Insomnia or excessive sleeping
Hair loss
Pale skin
Loss of menstrual cycle
Fainting spells
Dull eyes
Chronic sore throat
Looking tired or run down
Headaches

5 www.anad.org
6 www.anad.org

PSYCHOLOGICAL, BEHAVIORAL:
Depression, mood swings
Develops an obsession with all things food related, like reading recipes,
watching cooking shows, and memorizing calorie counts.
Begins to isolate from friends and social situations
Loses interest in hobbies and activities they used to participate in.
Talks about never feeling like they look good enough
Creates new rituals around food like only eating out of a specific bowl
or plate and eating alone.
Weighs and measures everything before eating it
Restricts calories or eats compulsively
Weighs him/herself often and is never satisfied by the number
Over-exercises
Hoards or sneaks food

WHAT CAN I DO?
The most important advice I can give parents is to LISTEN and ASK
QUESTIONS. If you feel that your child might be struggling with food
or body image issues don't hesitate to bring up the subject. She may not
be ready to talk to about it, but it will help just knowing that you will
be there if/when she is.

"My eating disorder problems started when I was 15 years old, but
I told my mother when I was 16. At first, she didn't believe me. We're
very close, but she had no idea that I was struggling so much. I actually
started making myself throw up so she'd know that I was serious. I think
that kids who are suffering with this WANT their parents to know about
it and want them to ask them about it. Even if they seem mad at first, it'll
feel good to be acknowledged. They'll feel safe. The way I see it, if you're
mature enough to make the decision to lose weight, then you should be
mature enough to discuss it with your parents. For me, my food issues
got worse when I was stressed and a lot of my stress came from school. It
was very difficult for me to open up about my food issues and a lot easier
to talk about school, so my mom would ask me questions about how
things were going at school and get me to share regular life stress. Being
able to talk about the things that were bothering me relieved some of the

stress I was feeling and I found that my food issues became less intense. I know that it may seem like kids don't want to talk about their problems with their parents all the time, but we really do need to know that they're there and that they care." Vikki, 22

Be prepared, it will be challenging. As parents we always want to fix whatever's broken in our children's lives, but this is a situation that will take hard work and patience from everybody. Let's face it, we all think our kids are fantastic, and it can be incredibly frustrating to hear your beautiful, intelligent children complain about how ugly and stupid think they are, and it would be very easy to just tell them they're being silly and move on, but they need more.

Vikki continued: *"When I'd tell my mom how bad I felt about myself she'd say, 'You're crazy. You're perfect just the way you are!' But all I'd think is that she's not really hearing what I'm saying, plus she's my mom, so she's supposed to say stuff like that."*

Tony watched his daughter battle an eating disorder from the age of 12 until she went into treatment a few years later. The struggle was difficult for the entire family. Being part of Sarah's treatment and recovery inspired Tony to become an outspoken advocate for children with eating disorders and is working hard to bring as much awareness to the problem as he can. He recalled: *"It is difficult to recapture the mindset and feelings that we had when my daughter Sarah was admitted to Sick Kids for treatment for anorexia in the winter of 2005. As a parent, we do whatever we need to to ensure that our children grow up healthy and in a safe environment. I recall feeling somewhat helpless, getting upset with Sarah whenever she refused to eat a meal or eat very little. The meal would usually end with an argument, and this would affect my wife and younger daughter. I recall that going on vacation was not always enjoyable; especially when it came to meal time, an argument would usually arise.*

Within a matter of six or so months, Sarah lost a lot of weight and a decision was made one day to bring her to Sick Kids. On the first visit she was not admitted as she did not 'qualify' as a patient, as her vital signs were not severe enough, according to the admitting nurse. A week later, she was admitted as she had deteriorated further: pale skin tone, cold hands, and a low heartbeat.

Sarah was hospitalized for about three months, and she recovered following months of therapy for the whole family. I remember going to see her almost every night after work, always feeling guilty as to what I could have done to prevent her illness or help her more to shorten her stay and help with her recovery.

We are thankful for Sarah's recovery, although a watchful eye is always there, fearing the worse of a relapse."

A few Dos and some Don'ts:

Do: hear what your child is saying. Make sure he knows that while you may not understand or agree with what he's saying, you do understand that it truly is how he feels. When you're dealing with negative body image, you're dealing with feelings over facts. There may not be any facts to back up what he's thinking, but his feelings are real and need to be acknowledged. Feel free to be honest about your feelings too by saying something like, "I hear what you're saying and I understand that this is the way you feel, but I honestly don't see you the way you see yourself and I wish there was something I could do to help you see yourself for the amazing person you are."

It's okay for parents to not always have the answers. Sometimes our kids even appreciate it when we admit that we don't.

Don't: try to trick them. If you're worried that your children are being too restrictive with food, it could become tempting to try to hide extra calories in what they're eating, and that's never a good idea. I can remember being 18 years old, and my stepfather telling me that certain foods were much lower in fat and calories than they actually were so I would eat more of them. Once I figured out what he was doing, I felt betrayed and started questioning absolutely everything he told me. Trust is so important between parents and their kids and we don't want to do anything that could weaken it.

Don't: Give in to every special food request they ask. Meal times are likely very stressful for them and in an effort to make things easier it may seem harmless to make them their own separate meal if what you've prepared for the rest of the family doesn't suit the food plan they've created. They may also want you to buy only foods that are fat-free and low-calorie. While we certainly don't want to add any more stress to what they're already feeling, we also don't want to encourage it. As always, focus on health. Instead of making two separate meals, make sure that the one you prepare is full of healthy ingredients and hopefully they'll try to join you. IF they really don't want to eat what you've made, it's okay for them to make something for themselves. But I strongly suggest that you encourage them to eat at the table with you. Isolation is common with eating issues and the more you can keep your child involved with the family, the better it will be.

Do: Get help! You cannot do this alone. Some parents might be afraid to tell anyone what's going on because they don't want to embarrass their children, or be perceived as having done something wrong themselves, but you need to ask for help. There are several resources you can look into. Start with your doctor. Be open and honest about what's been going on and ask if they've had other patients who have gone through the same thing. I can almost guarantee that the answer will be "yes." Get as many suggestions as you can. It may take some trial and error before you find a good match. Call your local hospitals and see what programs they may offer and if they can recommend any reading material that could be helpful. Go online! There are many online groups that are great for offering support and even more resources for you to try. Your child isn't the only one who needs help, inquire about support options for parents of kids who are struggling. Hearing that you're not alone can help ease some of the difficult feelings you may be dealing with.

Remember, even if your child isn't ready or willing to talk to someone about it yet, having done the research early just means that you'll be prepared if/when she finally is.

Don't: hesitate to ask for help from teachers/coaches. Our kids usually spend most of their time away from home at school or involved in afterschool activities. Make absolutely sure that their teachers and coaches know that privacy and confidentiality is a must, and then let them know what's going on. It's important for you to know what their behavior is like as well as understanding of what their eating habits are when you're not with them.

Do: remind your child that you love her and will do everything in your power to help her through this difficult time. Let her know that you are there for her if she wants to talk and will listen without judgment.

*EXTRA TIP: People battling negative body image or eating disorders, not only see things in a skewed way, but can also hear things in an entirely different way than they were intended, so be prepared to be confused. Even the most innocent of comments can come across as an insult to someone who is intensely focused on how she looks, and this can make simple conversations feel like a battle ground littered with landmines.

A few months ago, a woman in her 50s approached me at the gym looking very upset. She told me that she had bumped into an old friend of hers recently, who she hadn't seen in almost a year and that friend looked at her and said, "Nice to see you, you look great now."

I understood right away why she was upset.

What her friend said was, "Nice to see you, you look great now."

But what she heard was, "The last time I saw you, you were thinner. Now you're fat."

After explaining to her that it's never a good idea to create a subtext to someone else's comments and that she needed to just take the sentiment at face value, she was able to recognize that she was overreacting and promised to let it go. Having been dealing with her body image issues as long as she had been, she understood that she was being a tad oversensitive.

I can remember feeling the same way when I was struggling. In fact, I can remember a specific day when I was 20 years old and had met my mother and sister at a mall to do some shopping. When my sister saw me, she simply said, "You look good." That was it. But it was enough to bring me to tears! It sounds crazy, I mean how could the words, "You look good," be anything but a compliment?? Here's the thing, I knew that my food problems and weight loss were driving my sister nuts and that she was having a hard time watching me get thinner and thinner, so when she told me I looked good, I just assumed it meant that I had gained weight and the thought of that was unbearable.

Try not to stress over it. You can't walk around constantly worrying about everything you say. You may say the wrong thing at times and at times you may say the right thing and it will still come across as wrong, but don't worry. You're doing your best and that's all you can do.

STICKY QUESTION: *My 6-year-old seems to be overly concerned with how she looks and stresses over everything she eats. My friends say that all girls complain about their weight and that I'm silly to worry. Am I right to be concerned, or is she too young to have any real body image issues?*
SOLID ANSWER: *Sadly, there is no "too young" when it comes to low self-esteem or negative body image anymore. Statistics show that 42% of kids in grades 1-3 already wish they were thinner. While you don't need to panic, you do need to reinforce encouraging messages about your bodies and a positive environment around food. Keep watching—if you think that your child's anxiety around her body is increasing, it's time to seek help.*

STICKY QUESTION: *My daughter came to me and told me she thinks her friend may be obsessing over her weight and is worried about her. Should I get involved?*
SOLID ANSWER: *Yes. But first you need to get more information. Ask her why she's worried and ask for specific examples. If you are friendly with the child's parents, call them and let them know that you're not trying to be intrusive, but that you're calling out of concern, just to let them know about your daughter's concern. Be prepared, they may become defensive and have a kind of, "Not my kid!" response. If that's the case, then you've done all you can do and need to walk away. If you don't know the parents and you believe that she might be in danger, then tell a teacher or school principal just so someone is aware of what's going on. Keeping an open line of communication around this with your own daughter is very important. She needs to know that she can continue to come to you with her concerns if she needs to. There's also a chance that her friend might be angry at her for "snitching,, but she needs to understand that being a good friend sometimes means having to make tough decisions and that it's better to have an angry, but healthy friend, than one who's sick and suffering in silence.*
 Once you've spoken to the people who need to be told (parents or teachers), don't discuss it with anyone else. Gossiping is hurtful and will make it harder for her to seek help.

Chapter 12

What if mom is the one with body image issues?

"I think my mom feels really insecure about herself, because every time we go to take family pictures she always says she looks too fat." Kaitlin, 11

"My mom always compares herself to other people and my grandmother is always like, "Oh my God, look at my belly fat! I've got to get rid of it, I look DISGUSTING!" Jasmine, 10

"My mom has a ton of pictures of herself from her wedding day, so she compares herself to how she looked then because she was skinnier. But I always tell her that it's not how you look that matters, it's how you feel about yourself." Chloe, 10

"I think my mom feels bad about herself because she can't leave the house without having perfect hair and perfect makeup." Sarah, 11

We've already established that our society's obsession with "thinness" is affecting people of all ages and genders. And we know that moms are just grown up little girls whose experiences have helped them become the women that they are. But what happens when these experiences, combined with society's incredibly narrow perception of beauty turns into serious body image or eating disorder issues?

I talk a lot about the challenges that come from being a kid with body image issues or being the parent of one. Having been a teenager myself when my eating disorder issues started, I understand what it's like to be growing into a body that seems inadequate and I know what it's like to constantly wish to be thinner, prettier, smarter, funnier and more interesting. It sucks.

What I don't talk about as often, though it proved to be even more painful for me, was what it was like to have those feelings as a grown woman...with children. What made my eating disorder more disheartening as a parent was that it wasn't just affecting me, but was now impacting the lives of my children, and the guilt from that was hard to bear. While I'm grateful that my kids were young enough to be somewhat oblivious to the pain I was in, I'm also aware that while they couldn't understand what was happening, their version of "normal" had become somewhat warped and that was my fault. I battled my disorder during part of my teens, all of my twenties and part of my thirties. It finally reached a point where I had given up on myself. I was tired of fighting and feeling like every time I managed to pick myself up, life would sucker punch me in the gut. I was exhausted. However, even though I had given up on myself, I wasn't able to give up on my kids. Knowing how much they needed their mom, I knew I needed to find the strength to pick myself up one more time and find the help I needed.

Asking for help can be an incredibly difficult thing for a mom to do, because we're usually the ones solving other people's problems. For some reason, moms feel like they need to have all the answers and be able to fix every situation that comes their way, while making sure everyone in the family is well taken care of. What we need to realize is that we can't do it all. Even the people who get leaned on the most for support, sometimes need to do the leaning themselves, and that's OKAY.

I wasted too much time trying to cope with my food issues by myself and then feeling guilty because I was losing the battle. Guilt is not productive. When I finally decided to make some serious changes, I knew that it wasn't enough to just be a mother to my children; I wanted to be the best mother I could be. I wanted to be the type of mother that my mother had been to me. I wanted them to grow up remembering a house filled with music, dancing and a lot of laughing. Accepting that I couldn't make that happen on my own, I sought help.

It's important to note that I had a lot of missteps before I found a program that worked. I saw behavior therapists, psychologists, psychiatrists and pretty much every "ist" you can think of. But I didn't stop trying until I found a program that was right for me, which was a group recovery program, at a hospital, three nights a week.

Mothers want so badly to be perfect for their kids, but sometimes its okay for them to see our flaws. It teaches them that being imperfect is perfectly fine, and that's an important lesson to learn.

If you are struggling, if you know that you are not as happy as you want to be, tell someone. We're always trying to teach our kids the importance of liking, accepting and being proud of themselves, now it's time we start believing it for ourselves.

Nine signs that you may be a mom with an eating disorder (things I learned the hard way):

1. You avoid family functions because you don't feel like you look good enough and are afraid you'll be judged.

2. Your children think they have your attention while you're spending time together, but all you can think about is what you've eaten, what you're eating, and what you're going to eat.

3. On your way to a restaurant for dinner, your child asks, "Are you eating today, Mommy, or just watching?"

4. You find it difficult to walk to your children's bedroom at night to tuck them in, because you're either too weak from fasting or too full from binging.

5. You force yourself to go to the gym very early in the morning or very late at night, even when you're exhausted, because you feel awful if you miss a workout.

6. You discover that the child safety gates that your kids have outgrown are no longer packed away, but have been reinstalled by your husband so he could hear you sneaking downstairs to the kitchen at 2 am to make pancakes.

7. You've never been on a family vacation where a bathing suit was required. Ever.

8. You find yourself having to convince your kids that they did, in fact, already finish all their Halloween candy, while you hide the wrappers in your underwear drawer.

9. The foods that you're binging on, restricting yourself from, or purging over are keeping you from enjoying the life you deserve and want so desperately to have.

Here's the good news: Mothers are incredibly strong human beings, even when they can't see it themselves. We have a gut instinct that will keep us fighting for our children's well being, no matter what. It's this need to take care of our kids that gives us the courage to do whatever it takes to take care of ourselves as well.

Chapter 13
Schools: Education without humiliation

"Health education messages about overweight and weight control are likely to make young people feel worse about their bodies and themselves in general." Professor Jennifer O'Dea, Health and Nutrition Education, University of Sydney.

Childhood obesity is a growing problem in our society. We know this because we are constantly being told by newspaper articles and television commercials that our kids are just too fat. Some say it's because they're lazy and spend too much time in front of their TVs or computer screens playing video games, other blame all the fast food they consume. Whatever the reason, we are repeatedly being told that our kids are getting fatter and fatter and we need to intervene as quickly as possible. While I agree that childhood obesity is an issue right now, and I agree that something needs to be done to help our kids live healthier lives, I'm also aware that we need to be extremely careful in how we go about doing that.

Recently, the government has started to get involved by implementing obesity prevention programs into our schools. This might sound like a good idea, but don't be fooled: obesity prevention programs also tend to be focused on weight instead of health and the truth is that we really don't want our kids to be focusing on weight. Somewhere along the lines, we've managed to confuse being healthy with being skinny and the two are not always synonymous.

I love that schools want to get involved in our kids health, but while obesity prevention programs may sound good in theory, they can be disastrous when put into action. By putting a focus on food and weight, kids are becoming more anxious about how they look and the shapes of their bodies. In an effort to encourage healthy eating, many schools have banned "junk food" and some offer prizes to students with 100 percent healthy lunches. Let's face it, when you ban something or make it taboo, it only makes whatever it is seem more enticing. Telling kids they can't have any cookies, will only make them want them more. Bribing kids with prizes for snack-free lunches won't mean that they'll be coming to school without them, it just means that they'll hide their snacks in order to get their prize, then sneak away later to eat it in private. Hiding and sneaking food is not a habit we want to encourage.

One Friday afternoon last year, I was sitting in my car in front of my sons' school, waiting for them to walk out. As Logan, my 10-year-old, got into the car, he shook his head disapprovingly and said, "We had an assembly at school today and you are NOT going to be happy!" He then told me about the new Healthy Eating program being implemented at their school. Similar to many other schools, it involved the restriction of "bad" foods and awarded prizes for "good" ones. He was right; I wasn't happy. I had already been hearing from parents at other schools who had noticed a change in their children's attitudes around food since their schools had started their food programs. Dinnertime used to be when families would catch up on events of the day, but had now had become a source of anxiety over every calorie and fat gram ingested. I didn't want to see that happen at our school.

In my case, it took several meetings with school staff and an awful lot of persuading to have the program removed, but it was.

I believe that the intentions of these programs are to help our kids replace unhealthy behaviors with healthier ones and I truly appreciate the teachers who volunteer their time and effort to lead them. Most teachers are swamped with a curriculum that is more than a little overwhelming and I am very grateful to all the teachers who go the extra mile to continue to help our kids after hours. This is why I think it's unfair to them and to the students to promote a program that is so flawed. If our schools are really concerned about the health of their students, they need to do the research involved to ensure that they're not trying to solve one problem while inadvertently creating a new one. Obesity prevention plans tell kids how to avoid getting fat, but don't teach anything about the fact that healthy, fit bodies can look different from each other.

What are the risks for kids at the elementary school level?

1. Fear: Kids may become stressed over every calorie and fat gram they consume and will develop an unhealthy relationship with food and intense fear of gaining weight.

2. Schoolyard bullying: Too many kids are getting picked on at school already, without having the government tell them that they need to lose weight. All of the negative messages around size at school can lead thinner kids to tease the heavier ones. If we're telling kids that being heavy is "wrong" then they'll see nothing wrong with making fun of the kids who are bigger than they are.

3. Apathy from skinny kids: A lot of kids who are naturally lean, mistakenly believe that they can eat whatever they want and don't have to exercise to be healthy because, after all, they're already skinny.

4. Hiding and sneaking food: If kids feel embarrassed about what they're eating, they won't want to eat in front of people. By sneaking around with their food, kids end up dealing with feelings of shame and disgust with themselves. These feelings negatively impact their self-esteem and will put them at higher *risk for developing an eating disorder.*

5. Confusion over parental choices: When a parent packs his child a lunch for school, he shouldn't have to worry about a school staff member second guessing his choices and possibly removing something she deems "unhealthy." Children need to trust their parents, and parents need to feel confident that the decisions they make for their kids won't be overruled by their school.

"My daughter was in junior kindergarten and she was really skinny and I was happy just to get calories into her. She use to come home from school and tell me her teacher took away her junk food snack because of the "No Junk Food Policy" so she couldn't eat it. I used to find it funny because the teacher was like 300lbs and I used to think that the teacher was probably eating her snacks in the teachers' room. It made no sense to me at all because it just made her feel negative

about food! Why not just be positive about food and make nutrition part of the curriculum?" Karen, 34

"Negative consequences of the war on obesity are also being felt by normal weight children who incorrectly perceive themselves as being fat." Professor O'Dea

Not surprisingly, many students are so unhappy with all of the food rules and regulations, that they've started rebelling against them. According to several of the high school students I've spoken with, when the foods they like to eat are replaced with less appealing options, they just leave school property, head over to whatever fast food restaurant is nearby and fill up on the exact foods they're supposed to be avoiding. Teaching kids how to choose healthy foods is good idea, but making the choices for them just creates resentment.

In April 2012, two students from St. Thomas Aquinas Secondary School in Brampton, Ontario decided to launch a video protest against their province's ban on junk food. Student council members Samuel Battista, 18, and Brian Baah, 17, are vehemently against the ban as they feel that the government shouldn't be deciding what they can and cannot eat. By removing sugar drinks and fattening foods from school vending machines and cafeterias, students are left feeling like their school doesn't trust them to make proper decisions for themselves.

Samuel asks: *"At the end of the day, how can the government expect students to make the right choices, if the government themselves is taking away these choices?"*

Brian continues: *"We're basically being told that we're inadequate and unprepared to make our own decisions."*

Another frustrating part of this situation is that once again, health and weight are being confused. The students comment on the fact that while pop has been removed from their vending machines, it's been replaced with DIET pop! I'm not sure how the chemicals in diet pop are a healthier option than the regular kinds. The message these kids are getting is that the diet option is better because it has less calories, which is simply not the case.

When I spoke with Brian, he explained that what they wanted from their school was more education and less dictation. He said: *"We want schools to teach nutrition and healthy eating and then trust us to choose the foods that are right for us."*

Sherayah, 17, says: *"When my high school changed all the food they were offering, I asked my teacher why they were doing it and she just said it was because the school board told them too."*

How anyone could think that an answer like that would be satisfying is beyond me; that's pretty much the same as when a parent says, "Because I said so!" and when has that answer ever been acceptable to a child?!

The point is, schools have every right to offer healthy foods and discuss healthy living with their students and any effort to help them lead long, productive lives is appreciated. They just have to make absolutely sure that what they are doing really is what's best for the kids. We need to talk less about what's wrong with their bodies and more about all the things that are right! Instead of trying to get kids to fit the same mold, we should be teaching them that there is no mold and that being different from each other should be celebrated not criticized.

The way I see it, if we TELL kids what to do they just learn how to follow the leader. If we TEACH kids how to make their own decisions, we empower them to become leaders.

Kathy, a teacher with the Massachusetts school board shares: *"Healthy food is certainly a hot topic. Everyone is talking about improving school lunches and removing high calorie drinks from vending machines during school hours. The state also tried to ban the selling of cupcakes and other fattening foods at football games and as well as ban bake sales as fundraisers after school. There was a huge outcry from the public and that part of the changes was rescinded."*

WHAT CAN WE DO?
1. Talk to the school Principal as well as your child's teachers and ask them what rules or guidelines they have in place around food.
2. If you are uncomfortable with how the issues of food, health and weight are being handled, speak up! Let your concerns be known and feel free to ask for your children to be exempt from any programs you don't agree with.
3. If at any time, you hear about kids being negatively affected by food or health programs, share what you've heard with the school principal. If even just one child is being hurt, it's one child too many.
4. Be patient and understanding. This is a big undertaking! Expect some trial and error when it comes to finding programs that work.

5. Offer some healthy living suggestions of your own!
  - Pick a fruit/veggie week: Give each class a specific fruit they need to bring in that week, and then count how many of these fruits were actually brought in. At the end of the week, the classroom with the most fruits wins! Try the same thing with vegetables the following week.
  - Vitamin: Choose a vitamin and then ask students to bring in an item food containing that vitamin. This is a great way for kids to LEARN about food. The teacher can hang a list of food examples on the wall for the kids to choose from and then add them all up at the end of the week. Take Calcium for example, the list of foods could include: Yogurt, milk, cheese, salmon, tofu, spinach, peas, sesame seeds and broccoli. Healthy living and healthy learning!

Physical Education should not be optional
  Eat less? How about exercise more?
  While eating in a balanced and healthy way is important, it seems like some schools are focusing too much of their attention on getting junk food out and not enough on bringing exercise in. Kids spend most of their day in school and need a chance to move around, get their hearts pumping and muscles working. It's been proven that just 20 minutes of sustained moderate to vigorous exercise can help kids learn better.
  According to a 2010 publication by the CDC (Centers for Disease Control and Prevention):

"There is substantial evidence that physical activity can help improve academic achievement, including grades and standardized test scores. ... Increasing or maintaining time dedicated to physical education may help, and does not appear to adversely impact academic performance."

Teachers are under a lot of pressure to reach the academic goals they've been given and as a result, sometimes feel the need to cut gym classes short, or skip them completely in an effort to stay on schedule. Kids are being given the message that exercise isn't all that important and is something you do if you have the time. Sadly, this is an attitude that stays with them through high school and into college. It's no wonder they're feeling incredibly pressured to perform well academically and feel that making room for exercise is a luxury they can't afford.

Kathy continued: *"It seems like the trend is for less physical education classes and less recess time for the elementary school students. The cuts to Phys. Ed. are due to tight budgets and on having kids prepare for state tests on reading, math, etc. If the town is wealthy, of course the budget will be higher. Inner city schools have tight, tight budgets and are often built right on the street where it is unsafe to play and with no gym equipment to play with."*

Jordan, elementary school teacher, 7 years: *"Increased daily activity, can be encouraged through mediums such as lunchtime intramural activities, partnering with community agencies etc. With this in mind, you need truly committed teachers because these examples take a lot of time to plan for, organize and maintain."*

I understand the importance of an academic focus, but think that we are doing our kids a huge disservice by not putting an appropriate amount of importance on their physical health.

A study out of Queen's University in Canada revealed that 51% of female students between 18-25 years reported binge eating due to stress and pressure to succeed academically and stress is also known to increase the risks of heart disease. Interestingly enough, exercise has been proven to be a great stress reducer!

I realize that taking unhealthy foods out of schools is a lot easier than trying to fit more physical education into them, but all the professional and financial success in the world won't mean anything if you don't live long enough to enjoy it.

TRY THIS!

Some schools keep kids inside for recesses as a form of punishment for bad behavior. Don't be afraid to let your principal know that that's not an option for your children. Discipline is necessary sometimes and I have no problem with my kids being given extra homework to do in their free time if they've done something inappropriate or against the rules, but taking away their playtime doesn't work for me. Especially counterproductive is when kids who just can't seem to sit still are made to sit still in the school office during what would be the perfect time to release some of their pent up energy.

Our children need to feel supported at home and at school, and conflicting opinions between parents and teachers can result in some very confused kids. Parents want happy, successful kids and teachers have dedicated themselves to helping them get there and we all have a better chance of making that happen if we work together.

Chapter 14

Media madness and fat phobia

We are terrified of becoming fat. Fat has become the new "F-word" and for a lot of people, it's far more offensive than the old one. WHY are we so incredibly fat phobic? Fat, after all, is an essential nutrient that plays a vital role in maintaining healthy skin, hair and nails. It insulates our internal organs against shock by maintaining body temperature, promotes healthy cell function and serves as energy stores for our bodies. So why are we so afraid of it?

Maybe it's because every time we turn on the TV or flip open a magazine, somebody is telling us that we need to get rid of it! Once we're convinced that they're right, they are ready and waiting to tell us exactly HOW we should go about doing it; for a fee of course.

We hear it from 30-second commercials to 30-minute infomercials; from hour-long reality shows to celebrity hosted talk shows. The message is: Lose weight fast!

As adults, it can be difficult to ignore these messages. As a child, it's even harder. Having been around a lot longer than our kids have, we've become somewhat savvy to sneaky marketing ploys used by diet companies to get us to buy their products. But kids can be a lot more trusting than we are, simply because they still think that people on TV don't lie. Wouldn't it be fantastic if that were true?

The truth is diet companies will do or say anything to get our money because they care more about healthy profits than healthy consumers. We understand that, but our kids may not.

It can be very frustrating as a parent, to take the time to make decisions we feel good about concerning the programs that our kids watch only to be undermined by the "Lose 20 pounds in 10 minutes!" message that yells at them during a 30 second commercial break.

STICKY QUESTION: *What do I tell my son when he sees diet ads on TV and asks me if he needs to lose weight?*
SOLID ANSWER: *Simply explain that they are a company that is trying to make money and will only make money if they make you feel badly enough about yourself to buy what they're selling. Explain that the people in the ads are being paid to say the things they're saying and have no idea what's best for you.*

WEIGHT LOSS TV

"I couldn't believe it when my 11-year-old daughter came home from school and was upset because her teacher had been playing episodes of The Biggest Loser in the background during gym classes. Dalia said she felt sad for some kids because the teacher would yell, "Come on girls, move those chubby little legs!" I found out later that watching the episodes in class were impacting her self-esteem as well. She's never had any reason to worry about her weight, but just being in that class had her thinking she needed to be on a diet. The worst part is that it's two years later and they're STILL using it as "motivation." Cheryl, 42

Watching people lose weight has, for some reason, become a popular form of entertainment. When we're watching these shows it's easy to forget that we're watching real people with real struggles. Because we've become somewhat immune to watching people lose weight on our TV screens, we may not understand the impact they can have on our kids if they're watching them with us.

I've heard a few parents who watch these weight loss shows say, "I know it's ridiculous, but we just watch it because we think it's funny!"

Again, as adults we understand that the celebrity trainers are yelling at the overweight contestants because it makes for entertaining television, but how can we expect our kids to be kind to the heavier kids around them, if we're laughing at this kind of cruel behavior on TV?

In a phone conversation, Biggest Loser (season3) runner-up Kai Hibberd discussed her experience with the dangers of "quickie" TV weight loss: *"We were immediately thrown into extreme diet and exercise regimens and were forced to continue exercising even when injured. Although there were doctors and nutritionists on staff, we were*

100

told to ignore their advice and focus only on what our trainers were telling us to do. There was so much pressure to succeed at the finale that many contestants resorted to starvation, sauna sweat sessions that lasted hours and pure dehydration to be as thin as they could be. I left the show completely terrified of food and survived only on coffee and artificial sweetener until my family intervened. I live a healthier, more balanced life now, but the scars are still there."

If you're reading this and thinking, "My kids are safe because they don't want those shows. We only watch shows that are on kids' channels," think again.

If you've seen any of the preteen TV shows on the air right now, you've probably noticed how little most of the actors resemble actual pre-teens. 9 year olds look like they're 12, 12 year olds like they're 16 and 16 year olds, well 16 year olds are getting pregnant and starring in their own TV shows on MTV!

With the lack of "real" pre-teens for our kids to watch, they are developing a skewed perception of what they're supposed to look like.

"When I see girls on TV who are really, really skinny it makes me feel like I'm really, really, really fat!" Jasmine, 10

With so many of the little girls and boys on TV not looking like little girls and boys at all, it can make average, healthy kids feel inadequate.

Kaitlin 11: *"I used to want to look like the girls on TV. I used to want to be perfect like them, but now I know that nobody's perfect."*
Me: *"How old were you when you wanted to be perfect?"*
Kaitlin: *"I was 5 years old."*

What has so many little girls sucking in their stomachs and so many little boys flexing their muscles in the mirror? Maybe it has to do with the fact that several of the cartoon characters we've grown up watching have been given sexy makeovers and our kids are taking notice. When did our animated characters get so glamorous? An old favorite,

Rainbow Brite, has been given a thinner body and long flowing tresses; and same goes for Strawberry Shortcake. The people behind Dora the Explorer have decided to age her into her tween years with a new body and sense of style. Tween Dora has traded her sneakers for ballet flats and wears jewelry and makeup. While ballet flats may be perfectly comfortable to walk around in, I can't see how they wouldn't be limiting while on adventures. I also can't help but wonder if the map and flashlight in her backpack have been replaced with lip-gloss and a mirror. If the creators of the show feel that their young audience would prefer to watch an older, more mature Dora, we have to ask ourselves WHY that is? Why are kids in such a hurry to grow up and why are we encouraging it? With so many of the newer animated characters being created to look sexier and more provocative than ever before, our kids need to see a representation of themselves that is less about makeup and miniskirts and more about fun and adventure.

STICKY QUESTION: *My 7-year-old threatens to scream and cry in the middle of the store when I refuse to buy her the sexy shirt she saw that looks just like Hannah Montana's, what do I do?*
SOLID ANSWER: *Invest in a pair of earplugs and head home.*
When you get there you can explain that TV people dress differently than we do because they don't get to run around and play the way we can. Trying to look glamorous all the time makes it hard to have fun and be a kid and that's just boring! (Keep the earplugs handy; this issue will undoubtedly come up again)

TRY THIS!
Real or ridiculous

It's important when kids are watching TV that they're reminded of the fact that what they're seeing isn't a realistic representation of what kids actually look like. When all she sees are little girls who look like teenagers, she can start to feel like she looks way too young and needs to be reminded that TV's version of childhood is different from the rest of the World's.

The next time you're watching TV together, grab some family pictures as well as some pictures of her class pictures from school. Compare the pictures of the kids she sees on television to the pictures of the kids she knows in real life. Chances are that she'll find it reassuring to see how ridiculously kids her age can be portrayed on TV.

Magazine Manipulation

"Even I don't look like Cindy Crawford in the morning"- Cindy Crawford, supermodel (in people magazine, 1/11/93)

If the old adage is true, and a picture really is worth a thousand words, we can be pretty sure that some of the words attributed to the pictures in fashion magazines would be: Photoshop, airbrush, stylist, makeup, lighting, breasts, buns, hair extensions, lash extensions, lip plumpers and tummy tuckers. Followed by words like: deceive, scam, lie, swindle, shame, envy and money.

"The body type portrayed in advertising as the ideal is possessed naturally by only 5% of American females," Renfrew Center Foundation for Eating Disorders

Fashion magazines lie. They fill their pages with beautiful pictures of glamorous young women hired to sell us products that are guaranteed to make us look just like them. The truth, however, is that we can never look the way they do in their pictures because what we're looking at isn't real. Between the hairstylists and makeup artists working on the models and the photographers and editors working on their pictures, the women we finally see in the magazines are reformed, reshaped and revised versions of themselves. Unfortunately, there are still so many women who read these magazines and end up feeling worse about themselves afterwards.

In 2009, SELF magazine put season one American Idol winner, Kelly Clarkson on their cover with the words, "Stay true to you and everyone else will love you too" written above her left shoulder. Nice sentiment, but too bad SELF didn't believe it. Even though Kelly talked about feeling confident about how she looked, SELF decided to give her a digital makeover resulting in a noticeably thinner body. When readers complained, the magazine admitted to making the changes and felt no need to apologize for it.

When did natural, healthy bodies become so offensive and computer generated ones become acceptable and even expected?

The true crime here is the impact it's having on our kids. Advertisers understand that when a young girl reads a magazine with impossibly beautiful women on almost every page, her self-esteem decreases and her vulnerability to their heavy marketing tactics increases. Most teen magazines split their content between beauty, fashion and dating tips leaving little space for articles that inspire and empower young women in areas of school, work, friendships and their community. By focusing on superficial issues, girls are being taught that beauty is the most important attribute they can possess, which leaves them having very little faith in their capabilities.

Laura 41: *"I can remember being a little girl and flipping through the pictures of my mom's fashion magazines. Every single model seemed to have the same expression and similar body type. I would practice their expressions in the mirror and hope that one day my body would catch up. It never did. I'm perfectly happy with my healthy shape and weight today, but can still remember how sad those magazines made me feel."*

Gone are the days when kids had to share their mother's magazines. With magazines like Seventeen or the Cosmopolitan and Vogue offshoots, Cosmo Girl and Teen Vogue, they can read articles that are written just for them; or so you'd think. While the June 2012 issue of Cosmopolitan boasts articles like: "Wild Sex Stories" and "How to find a guy in June", their little sister counterpart is teaching tweens, "The secret to being a great kisser" and asking, "Are you too easy?" with their monthly quiz. Is there really that much of a difference?

It's not easy being a kid. It's even harder being a kid trying to deal with adult situations. With the world encouraging kids to act just like adults, we need to remind them of how exciting things can be if they spend their time enjoying where they are now, instead of wasting time trying to speed up the clock.

STICKY QUESTION: *My daughter likes to read magazines, but how can I be sure that what she's reading won't damage her self-esteem?*

SOLID ANSWER: *There are some great magazines available that offer a fun, educational and safe alternative to the fashion and flirty advice you're trying to avoid. An excellent choice would be New Moon Girls-- a magazine created by girls, for girls and is 100% advertising-free and is dedicated to helping girls honor their true selves.*
www.newmoongirls.com

TRY THIS!
Stand up. Speak out.

There's no feeling more empowering than speaking out about something you believe in. So many of us read things in magazines or see things on TV that drive us crazy with frustration and all we do is complain about it. There is an alternative. The next time you're watching television, listening to the radio or read an article in a magazine and you see an advertisement for something you feel is dangerously deceiving or just plain offensive, DO something about it!

Write a letter
Send an E-mail
Make a phone call

Tell your child what you're doing and explain the reasoning behind it. Encourage her to get involved as well! We are only as powerless as we let ourselves believe we are.

Internet

An estimated 7.5 million Facebook users are under 13 years old and 5 million are under 10 years old, according to the 2011 'State of the net' survey from Consumer Reports. The good thing about the Internet is that it enables you reach millions of people from around the world. The bad thing about the Internet is that it enables millions of people from around the World to reach you. And your kids.

The Internet is an amazing tool that gives us access to endless information on endless subjects and is constantly evolving to appeal to more and more people. Like it or not, our kids are using the Internet for everything from schoolwork to socializing, and while many social media experts aren't suggesting we ban kids from the Internet, they do caution us to be vigilant about monitoring their activity on it.

Facebook, for example, is a great way to keep people informed about what's going on in our lives and an easy way to stay in touch with people who live far away. But for a lot of kids, it can become a huge popularity contest. I find it really interesting and somewhat disturbing when kids barely in their teens have hundreds and even thousands of Facebook "friends". The scary part is when they feel the need to seek validation from all of them, which can become extremely dangerous.

12-year-old Riley explains the new Facebook game her friends are playing called TBH: *"Basically, you send a message out to your friends asking them to "Like" your status and then they know to leave a TBH comment. TBH stands for: To Be Honest. You're supposed to write TBH and then say something honest about that person. It should be things like, TBH: I think you're nice or TBH: You're really funny. But the truth is, it's usually something mean like, TBH: "The shirt you wore at school today makes you look fat!" I never play that game because it's just pointless."*

People tend to be a lot braver with their nasty comments over a keyboard than in real life, which opens the door to a lot of negativity. It's crucial that parents are aware of what their kids are up to. This doesn't mean that we need to be looking over their shoulders at all times, but they need to understand that their safety is more important than their privacy when it comes to social media.

"I go on Facebook almost every day!" Matt, 10 years old

If your children are on Facebook, make sure that they add you as their friend. This doesn't mean that you need to post comments on their walls (in fact, I'm sure they'd appreciate it if you didn't) but it's important for you to know whom they're talking to and what they're saying. Remind them that this isn't a question of privacy, since NOTHING on Facebook is private. If they're posting comments that they wouldn't want you to see, then they shouldn't be posting them at all.

While it's important for kids to learn how to make their own decisions as we can't expect nor would we want to decide everything for them, when it comes to the Internet, parents need to be involved and aware of what their children are doing.

106

Dr. Jennifer Shewmaker, Associate Professor of Psychology at Abilene Christian University, offers this important advice to parents on her blog **www.jennifershewmaker.com**: *"Using computer mediated communication lowers our guard and leads to what's called, "hyperpersonal" communication, where we tend to share more in different ways than we might otherwise. We lose the social cues that usually warn us when we're getting out of line, such as the other person's facial expressions.*

Add that to the fact that most children don't get proper training in how to treat people online and you've got a situation that's ripe for trouble. A 2007 report stated that more than 40% of kids between the ages of 13-17 have been bullied online (Harris Interactive Trends and Tudes, 2007). But it's important to note that more young adolescents and even pre-adolescents are starting to use social media sites such as Instagram and Twitter."

When asked how parents can best protect their children from online danger, Dr. Shewmaker said: *"Parents need to be sure that their child's account is private. Children should not be on Twitter, because there aren't the same types of privacy settings on that network as there are on Facebook or Instagram. Parents need to make sure that their child is only conversing with people they know in real life. Parents also need to watch out for hurtful posts and respond immediately by cutting off contact with that person. However, parents should not get involved in online conflict with adolescents. This is not the behavior to model for your child. Instead, have your child block the online contact and then respond the way you would with any bullying behavior. That usually means reaching out to the other parent or school officials. The key is that parents must stay connected to what their child is doing on social networks."*

When it comes to body image, there are some extremely dangerous websites out there that actually encourage eating disorders. These sites are referred to as: Pro-Ana (pro-Anorexia) and Pro-Mia (pro-Bulimia). They are a meeting place for people looking for "Thinsperation" in their quest for extreme weight loss. These sites claim to offer support for those suffering, but what they actually offer are dangerous tips and tricks on how to lose weight in the fastest way possible.

Patricia, 32: *"After I got married, I had gained some weight and was spending a lot of time on the computer for work. I had recently read about a young actress who had confessed to battling Anorexia and mentioned how she had found online websites that encouraged extreme weight loss. I was curious about them and started to do a little research. I ended up becoming obsessed with them for a couple of months. I felt powerful when I was starving myself and it felt like the sites were giving me energy. As strange as it sounds, I felt like they were supportive. I never participated in conversations, but printed out every tip and trick they suggested. They were always giving tips on how to lose the most amount of weight in the shortest amount of time. Secrecy is a huge part of Pro-Ana sites. They encourage people not to tell their friends and family what they're doing so that they become increasingly dependent on their "support". My family was no idea how obsessed with my body I'd become. After just a couple of months, I became pregnant and knew that I had to stop abusing my body this way. It's been a few years, but there are still times when I'm feeling just a little bit vulnerable or insecure that I'm tempted to look them up again."*

Pro-Ana sites can claim to be supportive, however the goal of a truly supportive environment is to help you find recovery, not lead you down a path of self-destruction.

STICKY QUESTION: *When is it okay to snoop where my child is concerned?*
SOLID ANSWER: *Snooping is allowed for safety, but not curiosity.*

I have always been very clear with my sons. I promised them that I would never disrespect their privacy just because I was curious about what they were thinking or talking about with their friends. HOWEVER, I have also told them that I would NOT hesitate to do WHATEVER I needed to do if I ever felt that their safety was at risk.

Kids want to be treated like adults, but ultimately need to feel that their parents will always be there to guide and protect them, even if they won't admit it.

For all of the websites we'd love for our kids to avoid, there are also some pretty amazing ones that are committed to encouraging and supporting them to grow up believing there are no limits to what they can accomplish.

The most important message I could leave you with is that our society's adoration of seemingly, aesthetically perfect people will not change overnight. What can change, however, is how much we let that impact how we feel about ourselves. We need to truly believe that healthy bodies come in ALL shapes and sizes and that how our bodies work, is much more important than how they look. It's only when we believe that for ourselves that we're able to teach our kids the same valuable lesson. Our kids need to understand that nobody has the right to tell them who they're supposed to be or what they're supposed to look like. Chasing perfection is just a waste of time and energy since perfection is just an illusion and reality is beautifully flawed.

Proud-to-be-me List

Kids are amazing. Their potential is endless and if we can nurture their self-esteem and give them the tools they need to believe in themselves and chase their dreams with vigor and passion, there's no limit to what they can achieve. We need to celebrate the unique individuals that they are, and even more importantly, teach them how to celebrate themselves.

I've asked some fabulous kids to share some of the things they believe make them so special, and then it's your turn to continue the list with your kids! Have Fun!

"I know I'm healthy and great just the way I am and I don't care what anybody else thinks." Logan, 10

"I love my energy and my personality." Faith 11

"I am strong, funny, smart and a good athlete." Daniel, 8

"I am just naturally awesome." Riley, 12

"I love my eyes." Finn, 4

"I'm a good hockey player and I'm proud that I scored 2 goals in soccer last week." Anthony, 7

"I'm awesome!" Gurtej, 10

"I like that I can be myself and no matter what people think of me, I will always be proud to be me." Chloe, 13

"I like that I am a nice person and I'm good at football." Kyle, 11

"I don't worry too much about what other kids in school think about what I am wearing, I just wear what I feel really comfortable in." Casie, 9

"I'm a pretty intense dancer and I like to perform. When I look at myself in the mirror I like the way I look because I'm me and I try to be the best me that I can be." Amy, 12

"I am a good dancer, a good singer and good at drawing." Kira, 4

"I think I am smart and I feel proud of myself when I give money to charity. I'm also good at math." Jamie, 11

"I love that I play hockey and that my determination has helped be make the honor role at school." Sydney, 13

"My mom is black and my dad is white so I'm caramel and I think that's pretty cool." Jayden, 4

"I'm gonna give it 110%, let's leave the 100% for everyone else." Chase, 7

"It doesn't matter if my face is all dirty because I'm beautiful on the inside...by my heart." Lexia, 4

"I think I'm a very good soccer player and runner." James, 6

"I like that I have no problems with my body and I'm healthy. I'm a good size and it helps me do the things I like to do." Isabella, 9

"I like myself because I am helpful to other people and very fun." Chloe, 8

"I like that I am healthy and strong enough to ride horses and clean the stalls. That's way better than hanging out at the mall, worrying about clothes and boys. I know that it's good for both my hearts, the one that beats and the one that loves." Jordyn, 11

"I'm awesome because I can make light of almost any situation. That's also what I'm most proud of." Suzy, 17

"I love that I am creative. My imagination is full of awesomeness." Maddy, 8

"I don't really care about what other people think of me and I'm very focused and determined when it comes to things that I think are important." Dylan, 13

"I am proudest of my dedication to Taekwondo. I am incredibly passionate about this sport, from competitions to meeting new friends." Crystal, 13

"I don't think I'm awesome. I'm just a regular kid who is talented at Volleyball. I'm proud of the person I'm growing into." Kallan, 16

"I like myself because I am amazing." Aaron, 9

"I like myself because I'm nice, and I'm proud of myself when I do something nice for someone." Ryan, 11

"I like myself because I'm unique, and I'm proud of myself when I accomplish my goals." Savannah, 12

"I can't pick one thing about myself that I'm proud of because I'm proud of everything I do." Jake, 9

"I don't care what people think about my weight and I don't give into peer pressure. Be good to yourself and you'll have a good future." Carlee, 12

"I love that I am smart, I am creative and I am athletic." Emily, 11

"I like singing and dancing and have lots of confidence." Violet, 6

"I think I'm pretty smart and fun to be around." Ruby, 8

"I can sing well and like to perform in front of people." Josh, 16

"I'm funny and creative and fun to be around." Matt 12

"I like that I'm my own person and that I don't just follow what other people do. I also think I'm funny and smart." Sarah, 13

"I'm cool because I'm strong and nice." Zack, 8

"I like myself because I have a reason to live because I am important and I am me and nobody can tell me different." Madelyn, 12

"I am proud of myself because I have achieved most of my goals, like getting a hat trick in hockey and getting chosen as the Most Valuable Player in my league. I am also proud to be one of the smartest kids in my class." Nathan, 9

"I believe that we need to be who we are and say what we feel. I'm proud to be ME." Emily, 11

"I'm proud of myself because I never give up and I can protect myself with Taekwondo. I like myself." Katherine, 6

"I love myself!" Daniel, 5

Sticky Questions / Solid Answers, Family Activities, Warning Signs, Pledges
(downloadable printouts at www.eifrigpublishing.com)

Sticky Questions/Solid Answers

Q: What do I tell my son when someone at school calls him "fat"?

A: *Reassure him that his body doesn't need to look like anybody else's and that healthy bodies come in all shapes and sizes. He should feel proud to say, "I am healthy and great, just the way I am!"*

Q: My daughter/son wants to buy a doll/toy some of her/his friends have but I don't approve of. What do I say?

A: *"I'm glad you have fun at your friend's house, but there are certain toys that I'm not comfortable with and would prefer not to have at our house." Give a short explanation of why you feel this way.*

Q: How can I explain to my daughter why she is going through puberty before/after most of her friends?

A: *Everyone goes through puberty at her own pace; some sooner and some later, but we all catch up in the end. It's never something to be embarrassed about or ashamed of. It's a good thing and should be celebrated.*

Q: How do I respond when my child asks, "Do I need to go on a diet?"

A: *Nope. Diets are not healthy. But we can all try to make better choices with the foods we eat to make sure our bodies are getting the healthy ingredients they need to help us feel our best.*

Q: What do I tell my overweight child when he asks, "Am I fat?"

A: *Acknowledge that his body may be bigger than some of his peers' but that that's okay as long as it's healthy, so you will work together with fun physical activities and healthy, yummy foods to feel the best that you can feel.*

Q: How should I handle it, when my child's classmate makes a comment about the fact that I'm overweight?

A: *Simply say, "Some moms are bigger, some are smaller. Some moms have blonde hair and some are brunettes, but we're all great moms and we all have great kids.*

Q: How do I handle it when my mother makes negative comments about my child's appearance?

A: *Be clear and firm about the fact that any kind of negative "fat talk" is not allowed. Remind your mom that your goal is to raise a child with the confidence and self-esteem that comes from feeling loved and supported, not judged or criticized.*

Q: Is my six-year-old too young to have body image issues?

A: *Sadly, no. But by reinforcing positive, encouraging messages and being a healthy role model, you can certainly help steer her towards a healthy body image. Keep watching though; you want to make sure that you are aware of her feelings so you can seek help if the situation becomes more intense.*

Q: Should I interfere if my child suspects one of her friends may be struggling with eating disorder issues?

A: *Yes, but only to a point. Find out more information, and if you feel comfortable, approach her parents with your concerns. Let them know you are talking to them out of concern and not judgment and then leave it up to them to handle it.*

Q: How do I explain all of the diet commercials on TV to my children?

A: *These are companies who are only concerned with making money. They will say whatever it takes to make us buy their products. They'll even lie. Just because we hear something on TV, it doesn't mean it's true.*

Q: My child is adamant about buying clothing I find inappropriate, should I give in?

A: *Not if you truly believe that they are inappropriate. Sometimes as parents we have to give in to the latest trends, even if we don't love them, but if the clothes are clearly too mature or improper, then stand firm. Explain that, like it or not, what we wear can convey an image that we do not want, and until she is a little older, she will just have to trust mom's guidance on this.*

Q: When is snooping on my child the right thing to do?

A: *Snooping is permitted when it's done out of safety and not curiosity.*

Q: Where can I go to find positive, healthy magazines and websites for my children?

A: *There are many great resources. Here is a good start:*

A Mighty Girl: *World's largest collection of books and movies for parents and others dedicated to raising smart, confident and courageous girls.*
www.amightygirl.com

Adios Barbie: *One stop body image shop for identity issues including race, size, media and more. Promotes healthy self-image for people of all cultures and sizes. "Think freely and live freely!"*
www.adiosbarbie.com

Beauty Redefined: *Identical twins who specialize in media literacy and body image activism. Helping females understand they are capable of much more than being looked at.* ***www.beautyredefined.com***

Dr. Jennifer Shewmaker's Operation Transformation: *Explores the messages the media sends to kids and strategies for confronting them. "We are not powerless, we can be the change!"*
www.jennifershewmaker.com

Hardy Girls Healthy Women: *Non-profit organization dedicated to creating programs that empower girls and women. Created with a vision of all girls experiencing equality, independence and safety in their everyday lives.* ***www.hghw.org***

Journey of Young Women: *Mentors girls on their path toward adolescence and womanhood. Teaching skills on how to take responsibility for their physical, emotional and spiritual well-being. Partners with the Boys Mentorship Collaborative.* ***www.joyw.org***

New Moon Girls: *Ad-free New Moon Girls is the supportive global community for girls' creative self-expression. Explores the world, develops empathy and confidence. Fully-moderated social network + magazine is the place for safe supportive online learning & fun. Parents' Choice and Golden Lamp winner.* ***www.newmoongirls.com***

Pigtail Pals and Ballcap Buddies: *A company who believes in a child's right to a childhood. A product line and advocacy group created by a mom who wants better for our kids.* **www.pigtailpals.com**

Princess Free Zone: *Offers an alternative to princess for little girls featuring such things as unique and fun t-shirt designs. The underlying message is about embracing differences and empowering girls by offering greater variety.* **www.princessfreezone.com**

Shaping Youth: *Amy Jussel is the founder and executive director of Shaping Youth, a nonprofit, nonpartisan consortium dealing with the impact of media and marketing on kids. Using the tactics of industry insiders, Shaping Youth is embedding innovative programs that promote healthier, positive values by using the power of the media turned on itself.* **www.shapingyouth.org**

SheHeroes: *produces educational video content that empowers girls to dream big, explore their interests and passionately pursue career choices in fields where women are under-represented.* **www.sheheroes.org**

Targeting Teens: *Providing observations, insight and activities that help teens see through teen-targeted marketing while helping them maintain self-esteem.* **www.targetingteens.com**

The Achilles Effect: *Discusses pop culture messages about masculinity, their impact on boys and the benefits of introducing more gender balance to boys' lives.* **www.achilleseffect.com**

The Mauve Dinosaur: *A friendly, feminist blog with a focus on promoting self-love and healthy body image while sparking conversation about the way women are portrayed in the media.*
www.mauvedinosaur.blogspot.ca

Toward the Stars: *A global online marketplace that focuses on products that empower girls as well as gender-neutral products that teach kids to focus on strength, confidence, values, ability and health.*
www.towardthestars.com

How I learned to wear a dress: *A blog "Where feminism meets real life (and heels are totally optional)"* **www.howilearned.net**

Family Fun / Self-esteem building activities:

1. "I AM ..." Alphabet Game

Take turns coming up with positive, encouraging adjectives about yourselves to finish the sentence. The last person to run out of words wins the game! For an added challenge, try choosing your words in alphabetical order.

2. Everyday heroes:

Discuss important role models in your lives, use pictures as prompts when possible. Focus on character over appearance. Visit heroes in your community and point out how different they look from each other.

3. "All about me" book:

Help your children create scrapbooks about themselves. Use pictures, drawings and whatever mementos you can find to celebrate all of their favorite things, including: hobbies, friends, family, songs, vacations, etc. The possibilities are endless!

4. Sunshine List:

Ask your child to share one thing at the end of each day that she's proud of and add to a list that you hang somewhere visible (refrigerator door, bulletin board). At the end of each week, read the list out loud, celebrate it, and add it to her scrapbook.

5. Body Swap:

Cut out pictures of adult models from magazines. Collect some pictures of your kids as well as other kids in their age group. Now cut and paste the heads of the kids onto the bodies of the adults to demonstrate how silly it would look of real kids had the bodies of the models they see in the magazines. Take this time to talk about how unrealistic it is to try and look like someone else and how important it is to accept and appreciate who they are.

6. Lunch Date:

Surprise your child at school and take her out for a special lunch, just the two of you.

7. Play Outside: homemade obstacle courses and Follow the Leader

Set up an obstacle course at your neighborhood park or even your own backyard. Get creative with your environment and use what's around you to jump over, run around or climb through! Play a lively game of follow the leader! Take turns leading and following.

8. Dance Party DJ:

Throw on your favorite music and dance around the room with your kids. It's simple and so much fun!

9. Dinner Theme nights:

Show your kids that healthy food can also be fun food. Designate one dinner a week as a theme night. Have your kids take turns coming up with interesting themes likes Japanese or Pajama night. Plan and prepare the meals together, it's a great way to create positive feelings around food.

10. Beautify your baby bump:

Grab some baby friendly finger paint and encourage your older children to create their very own masterpieces on your belly. When they're done, it's your turn to paint theirs! Take lots of pictures to make into a collage to hang in the baby's room.

11. Real or ridiculous - TV Time:

Pull out those class pictures and old family photos again and get ready to laugh at how different kids look on television than they do in real life. Point out how often the actors playing kids on TV are actually much older than the characters they're playing and all the ways that life on TV is different from reality.

12. Stand up and speak out:

Our kids need to believe that their voices matter. They need to trust how they feel and stand by what they believe. If they don't agree with something they see on TV, magazines or any other medium, they should be encouraged to stand up and speak out about it. Soft voices can still be powerful ones.

QUICK REFERENCE: Warning Signs

How can I tell if my child could be developing an eating disorder?

These are just a few examples of some of the signs your child could be displaying if she's struggling with an eating disorder:

Physical:
Weight gain or loss
Insomnia or excessive sleeping
Hair loss
Pale skin
Loss of menstrual cycle
Fainting spells
Dull eyes
Chronic sore throat
Looking tired or run down
Headaches

Psychological / Behavioral:
Depression, mood swings
Develops an obsession with all things food-related, like reading recipes, watching cooking shows, memorizing calorie counts
Begins to isolate from friends and social situations
Loses interest in hobbies and activities she used to participate in
Talks about never feeling like she looks good enough
Creates new rituals around food like only eating out of a specific bowl or plate and eating alone.
Weighs and measures everything before eating it
Restricts calories or eats compulsively
Weighs herself often and is never satisfied by the number
Over-exercises
Hoards or sneaks food

Important enough to mention again: These are just some of the signs that you may see if your child is struggling with food or body image issues. If you haven't seen any of the behaviors listed above but your instinct is telling you that something is wrong...go with your gut. Pay attention. Talk to your child and let her know she's got your support.

PLEDGES:

The following pledges are a good way to help your kids voice the ideas behind a strong and healthy body image. As always, it's important for kids to see their parents treating themselves with kindness and self-respect, which is why the body image pledge is an amazing promise they can make to each other.

(For the younger child and parent)

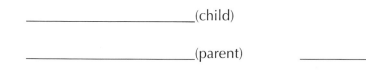

I promise to always treat myself with love and respect. I promise to be proud of who I am and not let anybody make me feel like I'm not good enough. I won't judge other people on how they look because it's what's on the inside that matters. I will believe in myself and follow my dreams. I don't have to be perfect. I'm great just the way I am. I don't need to be exactly like everybody else, because I am unique and special in my own way. I'm me and I'm magnificent!

_____(child)

_____(parent)   _____(date)

(For the older child and parent)

I promise to believe in myself and to reject the unrealistic and unhealthy ideals that may be thrown at me by society, the media, or marketers trying to profit off my bruised self-esteem. I will lead, not follow. I understand that nobody can make me feel bad about myself unless I let them. And I will not let them. I believe in myself and that I am amazing just as I am.

_____(child)

_____(parent)   _____(date)